TEACHER SELF-ASSESSMENT: A MEANS FOR IMPROVING CLASSROOM INSTRUCTION

Gerald D. Bailey

Analysis and Action Series

A National Education Association Publication

TEACHER SELF-ASSESSMENT: A MEANS FOR IMPROVING CLASSROOM INSTRUCTION

Gerald D. Bailey

nea
National Education Association
Washington, D.C.

Stock No. 1687–4–00

Note
The opinions expressed in this publication should not be construed as representing the policy or position of the National Education Association. Materials published as part of the Analysis and Action Series are intended to be discussion documents for teachers who are concerned with specialized interests of the profession.

Library of Congress Cataloging in Publication Data

Bailey, Gerald D.
Teacher self-assessment.

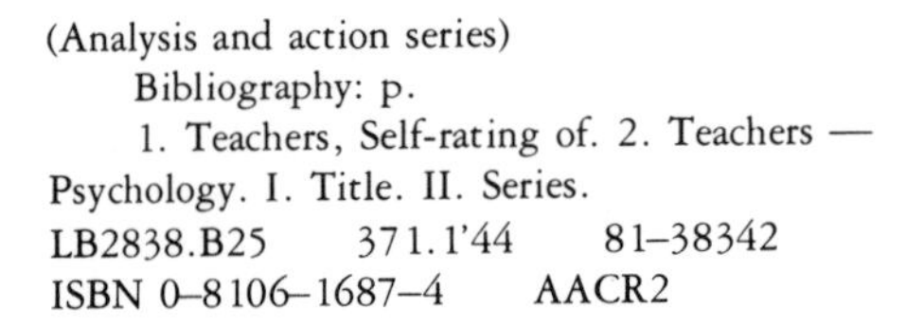
(Analysis and action series)
Bibliography: p.
1. Teachers, Self-rating of. 2. Teachers —
Psychology. I. Title. II. Series.
LB2838.B25 371.1'44 81–38342
ISBN 0–8106–1687–4 AACR2

CONTENTS

PREFACE

This text is intended for teachers who have two basic needs: (1) a need for a systematic and comprehensive approach to instructional improvement and (2) a need to become self-directed in their instructional improvement activities. The number of techniques and strategies available to the teacher in instructional improvement is extensive. Unfortunately, many of the instructional improvement techniques cited in the literature have been narrow in scope: that is, these activities have represented single approaches to instructional improvement. Second, almost all of the existing instructional improvement practices have required the teacher to be dependent on external assistance—from a supervisor or administrator.

The concept of teacher self-assessment, as it is presented here, represents a comprehensive approach to teacher self-improvement. The Seven Steps of Teacher Self-Assessment are a series of interlocking strategies that permit the teacher to identify and improve classroom teaching behavior. Although the steps are complementary and build on one another, they can be employed as individual strategies. Together, however, they represent a total approach to instructional improvement.

All of the ideas presented here on the concept of teacher self-assessment are the result of 10 years of informal and formal research with pre-service and in-service teachers.

The Author

Gerald D. Bailey, a former classroom teacher, is Professor of Education at Kansas State University, Manhattan.

The Advisory Panel

Virginia B. Di Cristafaro, Reading Teacher, South Miami Junior High School, Florida

Mary Louise Di Marzio, English and Remedial Reading Teacher, Raton Junior High School, New Mexico

Mildred Gamble, Language Arts Coordinator, St. Vrain Valley Schools, Longmont, Colorado

Charles E. Gobron, sixth grade teacher, M. A. Neary School, Southborough, Massachusetts

Ronald E. Gray, kindergarten teacher, Cole Elementary School, Cheyenne, Wyoming

Donald R. Nelson, Head, Teacher Education, Louisiana Tech University, Ruston

Alan T. Seagren, Assistant Vice Chancellor for Academic Affairs, University of Nebraska, Lincoln

Alice M. Shrewsberry, 11–12 Center teacher, Owensboro High School, Kentucky

Jerry Valentine, Assistant Professor, College of Education, University of Missouri, Columbia

THE ORIGINS OF TEACHER SELF-ASSESSMENT

For our purposes, *teacher self-assessment* will be defined as "the process of self-examination for the purpose of instructional self-improvement." The concept of self-assessment is one that almost all teachers are familiar with or have at least heard of sometime in their professional career.

Few people would argue with the statement that the ultimate responsibility for instructional improvement lies with the classroom teacher. Almost every teacher agrees with the concept of self-improvement, since the idea of continually upgrading instructional skills is at the very heart of professionalism. Unfortunately, very few teachers have been taught or trained in the specifics of teacher self-assessment. For many, the idea of teacher self-assessment is a state of mind—a process of mental reflection that occurs at the end of the day, week, month, or year. The use of self-assessment concepts in this publication is viewed as both a philosophy and a series of in-depth activities that lead to instructional improvement.

The concept of teacher self-assessment has its roots in three different educational endeavors: (1) supervision, (2) observation instrument development, and (3) teacher evaluation.

Marks, Stoops, and King-Stoops (1971), in their discussion of the nature of supervision, noted the importance of self-supervision in the following manner:

> The transition from imposed supervision, coupled with the desirable modern emphasis upon cooperative group endeavor, sometimes obscures one of the most important implications of modern philosophy and thinking in supervision; namely the possibilities for self-direction, self-guidance and self-supervision. The mature individual will not only serve as a leader in group enterprises and make contributions to group discussions and decisions; he often will engage in a program for self-improvement. (pp. 18–19)

Unfortunately, the wisdom of this statement did not spark a flurry of well-defined and concrete approaches that would allow the teacher to learn how to engage in self-help. Even the most current review of literature dealing with supervision reveals that minimal effort has been expended in the area of self-directed supervision or self-assessment practices (Sullivan, 1980; pp. 1–47). Irrespective of the lack of strategies, self-directed self-improvement has been perceived as an important concept by leaders in supervision.

Interest in self-assessment has also been generated by the historical development of observation instruments. The pioneer work of Ned Flanders (Amidon and Flanders, 1967) with Interaction Analysis gave substantial credence to the systematic study of teaching behavior. The perceived need for behavioral analysis systems was a natural outgrowth of the realization that prospective teachers would eventually operate independently in a school system, with few opportunities for external, objective feedback about their own teaching behavior. The flavor and importance of self-analysis was characterized by Amidon and Flanders (1967):

> The teacher . . . is continually exerting influence on the children and on the learning situation. . . . By studying his own behavior in some systematic, objective manner, the teacher may gain further insight into his own pattern of influence. As he gains insight into his behavior, he may decide . . . that he wants to change his behavior because he is not achieving what he has decided he wants to achieve on the basis of new insights about how children learn. (p. 72)

Researchers in the area of observation instruments, such as Rosenshine and Furst (1973), Medley (1979; pp. 11–27), Soar (1972), and Brophy and Evertson (1976), have sought to determine the value and results of the use of observation instruments. However, the subsequent bulk of research done with observation instruments has been along the lines of establishing the relationship between teacher behavior and student learning rather than exploring the use of observation instruments as a tool for self-assessment practices.

The third educational endeavor that has stimulated interest in self-assessment is teacher evaluation. Teacher evaluation is a distinct portion of the accountability movement and has become a highly controversial topic. The issue of documenting teacher efficiency and effectiveness continues to prey on the minds of teachers, administrators, and school district patrons. The current scene as it relates to teacher evaluation was summed up by Wiles and Bondi (1980) in the following manner:

> The present emphasis on teacher evaluation has come out of a decade of teacher unrest and lack of satisfaction by legislators and school board members with the system in which all teachers are

assumed to be equally competent to teach just because they have licenses or credentials. (p. 240)

In response to the demands placed on them, teachers and teacher organizations have argued for the right to help decide what kind of criteria should be used in determining quality in teaching and learning. As a consequence, the issue of being able to identify personal, effective teaching behavior has become extremely important to teachers.

Both researchers and practitioners have perceived a definite need for self-assessment practices as a method of instructional improvement. Unfortunately, techniques and strategies for self-help have remained fragmented and disjointed. The concept of teacher self-assessment, as presented here, attempts to weld several strategies together to make self-help a comprehensive enterprise.

WHAT IS TEACHER SELF-ASSESSMENT?

Earlier, self-assessment was defined "as the process of self-examination for the purpose of instructional self-improvement." At this point, the definition of teacher self-assessment can be expanded to be "the process of self-examination in which the teacher utilizes a series of sequential feedback strategies for the purpose of instructional self-improvement."

The basic assumption in teacher self-assessment is that the teacher can function in an autonomous fashion in self-improvement activities. The teacher's ability to function in a self-directed manner is contingent upon acquiring a series of self-help skills or strategies. The purposes of teacher self-assessment are to enable the teacher to—

- Become aware of personal classroom teaching effectiveness.
- Learn how to control classroom instructional behaviors.
- Become self-directed in instructional improvement activities.

Understanding teacher self-assessment can be accomplished by viewing the self-assessment approach as an organized, step-by-step process. Self-improvement comes about when a teacher acquires a series of competencies that permit intelligent decisionmaking about personal classroom teaching. There are basically seven different steps of self-assessment. Each step allows the teacher to become better equipped to assess teaching performance. Each step attempts to build on the next step, and the steps are sequenced in a simple to complex relationship (see Figure 1).

Figure 1
AN ORGANIZATIONAL APPROACH TO UNDERSTANDING AND USING TEACHER SELF-ASSESSMENT

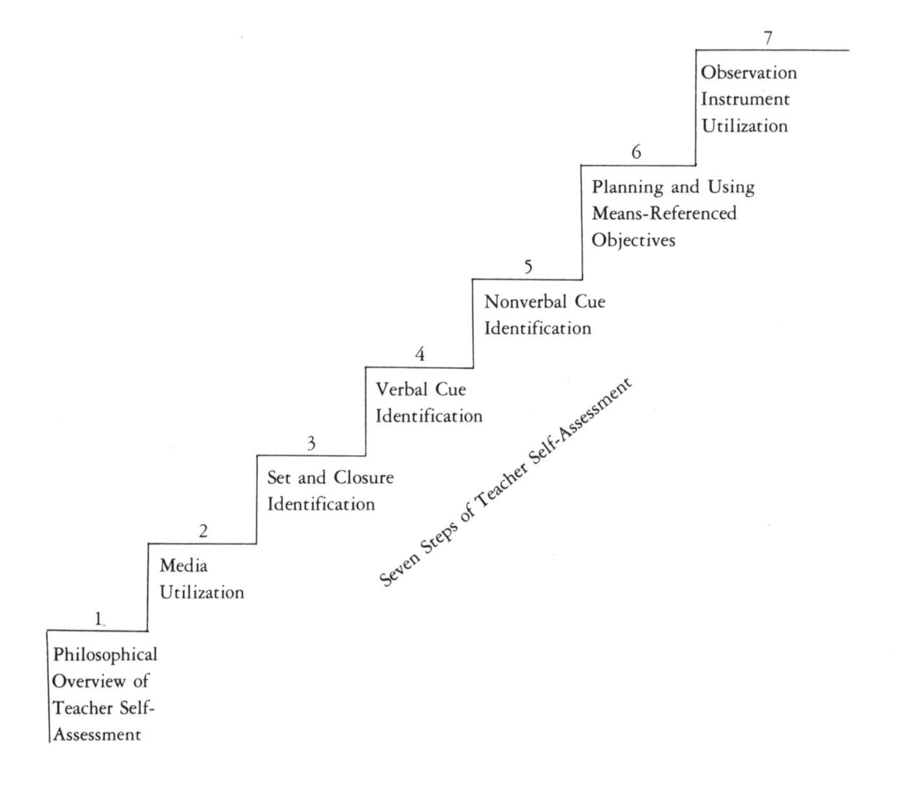

RESEARCH RELATING TO TEACHER SELF-ASSESSMENT

Research studies relating to teacher self-assessment, as the term is defined here, are virtually nonexistent. While this statement may alarm some readers, it is important to remember that teacher self-assessment is in its early stages of development.

To say that there are no research studies related to teacher self-assessment, however, would not be totally accurate. There are a number of research studies related to isolated self-help strategies. However, these studies have looked at such strategies as videotape feedback, self-perception, observation forms, without regard to the strong philosophical foundation and underlying principles needed to make teacher self-assessment functional for the classroom teacher. In short, researchers have tended to view a single strategy as the total process involved in teacher self-assessment. Researchers have not viewed the strategy in the context of a comprehensive understanding of teacher self-assessment.

An equally aggravating difficulty observed in the research is that authors have defined the term in many different ways. Bailey (1978) defines self-assessment as the practice of self-examination for the purpose of self-improvement. Specifically, this involves a process of self-examination that includes a series of seven interrelated steps that allow the teacher to engage in in-depth, long-term self-improvement.

Other authors, including Centra (1979) have defined self-assessment as the process by which teachers "rate their effectiveness on a scale form or provide a brief written evaluation of their teaching performance." (p. 48) In his survey of the literature on self-evaluation, Levin (1979) defined self-evaluation as the process "which involves improvement of instruction through having teachers reflect on their own teaching and modify it accordingly." (p. 243) These latter two definitions are indicative of the narrow scope that educators have given self-assessment, that is, *a mental reflection process that involves the use of worksheets or checklists.* Hence, a review of the literature as it relates to these limited definitions can be somewhat misleading to the teacher.

The Value of Self-Assessment

Peripheral studies relating to teacher self-assessment do not paint a bright picture for the classroom teacher. McNeil and Popham (1973) made this point very clear:

> We would like teachers to be students of teaching, systematically assessing and revising their own teaching behavior. Theoretically, persons want to evaluate themselves in order to obtain an accurate picture of their own abilities . . . but there are only a few studies indicating that some teachers are self-directing in their learning and expend effort in judging their behavior on the basis of the consequences of their teaching as revealed by the actions of pupils. Not having received training on how to focus on relevant aspects of their work, most teachers tend to criticize superficialities—personal mannerisms, appearance, voice and use of materials. Most teachers require others "to make them honest" and help them with their instructional problems. (p. 232)

Peck and Tucker (1973) drew much the same conclusion about the ability of teachers to become self-directed in instructional improvement when the authors discussed the aspect of providing feedback to teachers:

> The available evidence all indicates that teachers use such feedback to make instructive change in their teaching style only if another person participates in the feedback session. Apparently, simply looking at one's own performance does not lead to much new insight as to what one is doing, or else it does not provide adequate motivation to alter that pattern. The presence of another human being adds a potent factor which does induce positive change. (p. 947)

Peck and Tucker are adamant that teachers are largely incapable of personal objectivity and lack the motivation in the area of self-help.

A more positive conclusion was drawn from the author's own research. A five-year followup study of approximately 200 teachers revealed positive outcomes of self-assessment. The teachers involved in the study had had previous training in the Seven Steps of Teacher Self-Assessment. Those teachers (1) remained competent in self-assessment skills and (2) continued to value specific strategies of self-assessment. However, the teachers were found to engage in fewer actual self-help sessions than they did during the period of formal training (Bailey, 1980).

The Use of Media in Self-Help Practices

The use of media as it relates to teacher self-help has probably received more attention than any other strategy. MacGraw (1966) found that 35mm time-lapse photography is an effective technique for changing the behavior of student teachers.

Fuller and Manning (1973) reviewed over 300 studies involving self-analysis through the videotape medium. They concluded that videotape feedback has the potential to both assist and damage teaching performance. Exposure to videotape feedback under forced (adverse) conditions was not likely to produce appropriate changes in teaching behavior. An interesting finding was that audiotape feedback is less threatening to teachers than videotape feedback, but it is also less motivating.

Fuller and Manning (1973) also concluded that the presence of peers or a supervisor is more likely to produce significant change in teaching behavior. Support for this position can be found in studies by Fuller, Veldman, and Richek (1966), Morse, Kysilka, and Davis (1970), and Tuckman, McCall, and Hyman (1969). All of these researchers found that there was limited optimism for self-directed instructional improvement without the presence of a supervisor or administrator.

Teacher Attitudes Toward Self-Help

Various studies have shown that teachers have not been overly optimistic about self-assessment because of its strong association with evaluation practices. Wolf (1976) found that teachers have not generally been encouraged to evaluate their classroom behavior. As a consequence, self-evaluation is unlikely to occur or even be a productive enterprise.

Neely (1973) studied the attitudes of teachers toward self-evaluation. Although his study was confined to teachers in one state, an interesting finding was that teachers' attitudes toward self-evaluation ranged only from neutral to slightly favorable. In short, Neely did not observe a high degree of enthusiasm for self-evaluation among teachers.

A critical dimension of teacher self-assessment is the ability to accurately discern personal teaching qualities (self-perception). Unfortunately, the research in this area is equally unencouraging. Goodlad and associates (1970) found a discrepancy between perceptions of classroom observers and teachers' self-perceptions. Steele, House, and Kerins (1971), Bailey (1972), Weiss (1973), Walberg and Thomas (1972), and Solomon and Kendall (1976) concluded that teachers do not have a totally accurate perception of their instructional abilities.

Although these research findings related to self-perception are not encouraging, the reader must remember that the teachers studied were not trained in identifying their own instructional performance, nor were they made aware of instruments needed in studying their own classroom behavior. Therefore, it is realistic to expect that a classroom teacher's self-perception will not be totally reliable.

The review of the literature suggests a continuing need to define the concept *teacher self-assessment* when studying the effectiveness or ineffectiveness of self-help. Future research must focus on the result of training teachers in a comprehensive self-assessment program rather than on isolated strategies that could be considered important in teacher self-assessment. Preliminary research does not totally negate teacher self-assessment as a viable approach to self-help; however, subsequent research must be based on a conceptual framework that encompasses the total process of teacher self-assessment. The purpose of this book is to provide this conceptual framework for both practitioners and researchers.

STEPS IN TEACHER SELF-ASSESSMENT

STEP 1: GAINING A PHILOSOPHICAL OVERVIEW BY EXAMINING THE MYTHS SURROUNDING TEACHER SELF-ASSESSMENT

Although supervision, observation techniques, and teacher evaluation can be credited with setting the stage for teacher self-assessment, it would be less than accurate to say that the state of the art reveals a coherent movement. The Seven Steps of Teacher Self-Assessment suggest that self-help is a comprehensive, detailed approach; yet, few school districts have implemented the concept, nor have large numbers of teachers engaged in self-assessment practices. There appear to be a number of reasons for the slow development of teacher self-assessment. One of the basic explanations is that there are a number of myths or misunderstandings concerning self-assessment practices that have hindered the practitioner from adopting and embracing them.

Myth 1: Teacher evaluation and teacher self-assessment are synonymous practices.

Prevailing opinions of educators suggest that instructional improvement comes about from a larger act known as evaluation. That is to say, educators believe that the reason for evaluation is improvement of instruction. Many school administrators, when asked why they evaluate teachers, will indicate that the purpose of evaluation is to assist teachers in improving their instruction. Evaluation as a method for improving instruction has some merit. Greater strides in instructional improvement can be made, however, by having teachers engage in activities totally aimed at improvement of instruction rather than by using evaluation as a vehicle to improve instruction (Valentine, 1978). It is for this reason that teacher evaluation and teacher self-assessment must be treated as two distinct activities and should be viewed as serving two different purposes.

The advocation of separating teacher evaluation and improvement of instruction does not remove or diminish the need for or the value of teacher evaluation. Teacher evaluation is the process of an external observer (administrator or supervisor) obtaining information about a teacher's classroom performance in an effort to determine the value or worth of that teacher's classroom performance. The process of evaluation usually results in the external observer's labeling the teacher's behavior as satisfactory or unsatisfactory. The data generated from this type of evaluation are better used for retention, merit pay, salary increments, promotion, or other similar purposes. It is important to remember that instructional improvement does not have to be a part of this evaluation process.

What happens if the teacher fails to distinguish teacher evaluation from teacher self-improvement? The process of teacher evaluation can interfere with or retard the progress of improvement of instruction. Two major obstacles are encountered when evaluation and improvement of instruction are viewed as synonymous activities:

1. Many teachers perceive evaluation as a threat, since it ultimately involves administrative judgment concerning a teacher's worth or value. When teachers are threatened, the atmosphere leading to instructional improvement is dramatically diminished.
2. Teacher evaluation activities require the collection of information to form a value judgment concerning the teacher's competency. As a consequence, the evaluator spends much

time documenting opinions rather than sharing information with the teacher and assisting the teacher in personal efforts to improve classroom instruction.

The problems associated with viewing evaluation and improvement of instruction as identical concepts are substantial. Only when teachers can pursue self-improvement without fearing that someone else is judging their quality can they make the greatest gains in instructional improvement.

Myth 2: Teacher self-assessment is a method of self-improvement that is best learned through personal experience or by trial and error.

There is no doubt that some teachers learn how to engage in self-help as they gain experience in the classroom; however, specific techniques and strategies critical to the practice of self-assessment are seldom learned through experience. If this were true, the generalization could be made that people in any occupation need little job-related education; they can simply be placed on the job and allowed to learn from their experiences. Competence in teacher self-assessment comes about from reading, analyzing, and applying self-assessment in a systematic fashion.

Myth 3: Quality teacher self-assessment materials are easy, simple, and short.

There are a host of educational materials wearing the banner of self-help. A close examination of these materials reveals that they do not relate directly to the primary responsibilities of classroom teaching. These materials often relate to personal, social, or ethical behavior or go beyond the scope of classroom instruction. Many of these exercises are interesting, but few of them deal with detailed skills, behaviors, or strategies that relate to classroom teaching behavior and student learning behavior.

A common example of these self-help materials is a checklist or true-false reaction statement. Such an exercise often asks the teacher to reflect on past experiences and assign points to them. The teacher is then asked to calculate the total number of points, which is used as a classification or categorization of teacher effectiveness. These activities are obviously simple and short. Unfortunately, the majority of these reaction or checklist exercises rarely provide information needed to understand and classify behaviors associated with effective teaching. Equally important, they seldom supply information that can help teachers modify ineffective teaching behaviors. These exercises rely totally on subjective interpretations of the teacher.

Teacher self-assessment entails much more than the use of simple checklist activities that rely on personal reflection. The process of self-improvement requires objectivity and exacting tools that show teachers explicitly what is occurring as they teach. Teacher self-assessment provides precise methods that indicate how instructional behaviors can be kept or changed. Meaningful self-assessment materials are rarely simple and short.

Myth 4: Personal reflection is an effective strategy in teacher self-assessment.

A common strategy found in self-help materials is having the teacher reflect on previous classroom experiences and instructional behavior. The teacher is seldom aware of the nature of personal reflection. When a teacher is asked to reflect on personal past teaching behavior, it is not indicated whether this past behavior occurred yesterday, last month, last year, or 10 years ago. A compounding problem is that the teacher is rarely told which of the following this past classroom behavior should be compared with: (1) the ideal self, (2) other teachers, or (3) all teachers. Therefore, materials that emphasize a reflection strategy are not reliable or systematic.

Quality teacher self-assessment materials encourage the teacher to concentrate on current teaching behavior and use objective means to accurately identify this behavior. The audiotape recorder and the videotape recorder are two media tools that allow a greater degree of objectivity in analyzing the instructional self.

Myth 5: Teacher self-assessment is easily defined in breadth and depth.

One of the major reasons for the slow development of teacher self-assessment as a major movement is that people have tended to perceive self-help as a single approach or strategy. Historically, teacher self-assessment has not been viewed as a multifaceted or comprehensive approach. Previous attempts at defining teacher self-assessment have tended to emphasize one strategy (i.e., videotape or Flanders' Interaction Analysis Categories). Experts in the area of instructional improvement have been overly zealous in promoting the use of one method as a way of becoming autonomous in improvement of instructional activities.

Myth 6: Teacher self-assessment is a short-term activity.

Probably the most difficult concept to understand is that teacher self-assessment is a regular, ongoing process and rarely operates effectively as a short-term or single-time activity. The process of self-examination is sufficiently complex that few teachers are able to engage in meaningful instructional improvement by only spending a few moments before or after class or at the beginning or end of the school year. This type of sporadic self-examination basically destroys the concept of instructional improvement as a systematic and orderly process.

Teachers commited to self-assessment as an approach to professional development need to see the necessity of regular assessment periods that require time and patience. It may not always be convenient to create the regular schedules and find the personal patience and intrinsic motivation necessary for self-assessment. As a consequence, considering self-assessment as a long-term activity becomes exceedingly difficult.

Myth 7: Objectivity is impossible to achieve in teacher self-assessment.

Although complete objectivity is a lofty goal in self-help exercises, there are numerous strategies that can be used to maximize objectivity for the purpose of improving classroom instruction. Subjectivity can be kept at a minimum with the use of (1) an audiotape or videotape recorder, (2) observation instruments that capture teacher behavior in a systematic fashion, and (3) multiple sources of information concerning teacher behavior. Efforts aimed at minimizing subjectivity are extremely important in teacher self-assessment.

Myth 8: Effective teaching is impossible to identify in teacher self-assessment practices.

Debate concerning the nature of teacher effectiveness has raged over the last 40 or 50 years and will likely continue in the future. It is evident that educators have become more proficient at differentiating effective teaching behavior from ineffective teaching behavior; however, even the most recent literature surveys concerning teacher effectiveness suggest disagreement in research findings (Peterson and Walberg, 1979). This disagreement regarding what constitutes effective teaching prevents some teachers from actively engaging in self-assessment. In short, if the experts cannot agree on the characteristics of an effective teacher, why should the teacher be concerned about personal effectiveness? It is important to recognize, however, that *the success or lack of success of teacher self-assessment does not totally hinge on whether researchers can identify effective teaching.*

Research concerning teacher effectiveness is important, but the essence of teacher self-assessment is not the wholesale adoption of research findings related to effective teaching. Teacher self-assessment is, first, the ability to identify what is included in the teaching act. Second, teacher self-assessment involves analysis of the cause-and-effect relationship between teacher behavior and student behavior. Third, self-assessment involves the process of drawing conclusions about the effectiveness or ineffectiveness of personal classroom performance. The research findings reported in the literature cannot and should not be adopted by a teacher unless a careful step-by-step approach of self-examination is employed as the principal vehicle for instructional improvement. Research findings should be viewed as a frame of reference in teacher self-help rather than as a model to be incorporated in personal teaching.

The myths concerning teacher self-assessment are not likely to be completely dispelled for a number of years. However, if teacher self-assessment is to develop a strong following, many of the prevailing myths and misunderstandings regarding it must be challenged. When these myths are challenged and dispelled, teacher self-assessment will achieve the recognition that it deserves.

STEP 2: USING MEDIA IN TEACHER SELF-ASSESSMENT

One of the major building blocks in teacher self-assessment is the use of media. Access to and utilization of media are critical because of the need for objectivity in self-assessment (Peck and Tucker, 1973; pp. 945–47). Without some recording device, the teacher must rely on memory when engaging in self-analysis. Used in isolation, memory is one of the least effective techniques in self-help activities. Misperceptions of actual teaching performance are not uncommon (Bailey, 1972, Hook and Rosenshine, 1979). As a consequence, the use of media minimizes the degree of subjectivity that creeps into the self-examination process. There are a number of basic considerations that need to be addressed in the use of media for self-assessment practices.

Deciding to Use the Audiotape Recorder or Videotape Recorder

The audiotape recorder captures only verbal cues; the videotape recorder captures both verbal and nonverbal cues. The strengths and weaknesses of the audiotape recorder and videotape recorder as they relate to the process of self-assessment can be evaluated with relative ease. If a teacher is in a position to make a choice between the two media forms, the scoring system found in Figure 2 can be used. By looking at the characteristics of each form in the two columns and placing a plus (+) for a strength or a minus (−) for a limitation, the teacher can compare the advantages and disadvantages of each media form in regard to the teacher's personal situation.

Teachers generally have more difficulty operating the videotape recorder. However, the advantages of using a device with both audio and video capabilities over using one with only audio capability may be the single most important consideration. As a consequence, teachers must keep this in mind as they consider the scoring system.

Figure 2
SCORING STRENGTHS AND WEAKNESSES OF THE VIDEOTAPE AND AUDIOTAPE RECORDER IN TEACHER SELF-ASSESSMENT

Directions: Place a plus (+) for a strength or a minus (−) for a limitation in each area associated with the type of media: audiotape or videotape recorder.

Videotape Recorder	*Audiotape Recorder*
__ 1. Audio and video qualities	__ 1. Audio qualities
__ 2. Large	__ 2. Small
__ 3. Setup time: approximately 10–15 minutes	__ 3. Setup time: less than 5 minutes
__ 4. High visibility to students	__ 4. Low visibility to students
__ 5. Permanent record	__ 5. Permanent record
__ 6. Moderately portable	__ 6. Highly portable
__ 7. Moderately expensive	__ 7. Relatively inexpensive
__ 8. Mechanical operation, fairly complex	__ 8. Mechanical operation, fairly simple
__ 9. Accessibility	__ 9. Accessibility
__ TOTAL SCORE	__ TOTAL SCORE

Knowing the Operation of Audiotape and Videotape Recorders

When a teacher allows another person to operate recording equipment, the presence of that individual in the classroom can foster an artificial atmosphere. Interaction between the teacher and students is often affected when a third party is present. For this reason, it is essential that the teacher learn the mechanical operation of the media equipment.

Operation of the audiotape recorder should not present any major logistical difficulties for the teacher. However, self-operation of the videotape recorder presents some distinct difficulties and limitations. Such operation of the videotape recorder necessitates turning the equipment on record mode and allowing it to operate independently. As a consequence, the teacher will not be able to capture all of his or her physical movement and specific student interaction activity. If an operator is employed, the operator can focus on specific teacher and student interaction. The limitations of stationary equipment must be weighed against the limitations of having a camera operator in the room. If the camera operator does not represent a disruptive force, the assistance of this person is highly desirable. However, if the camera operator presents a conscious or unconscious disruption for the classroom, the teacher may find it more desirable to operate the equipment himself or herself.

Making Media Equipment Operational Prior to Actual Taping

Pretaping media activities can be as important as the actual audiotaping or videotaping. First, advanced setup can minimize potential damage done to equipment by students coming into the classroom. Student traffic around the equipment should be minimized whenever possible. Second, early setup and arrangement of equipment prior to student arrival prevents loss of valuable instructional time when class begins. Third, prearrangement of equipment decreases considerable student curiosity about the equipment. The teacher is able to proceed without giving undue attention to the equipment, and this precaution minimizes the potential for unnatural student reaction to the audiotape or videotape equipment.

One of the most important reasons for the prearrangement activities is to ensure that all recording elements are functioning properly. Testing audiotape or videotape equipment for approximately 10–20 seconds should be a common practice. Equipment checkout may appear to be a mundane procedure, but failure to ensure audio and/or video quality can be a costly and time-consuming error. Mechanical failure over a period of time can cause the teacher to become frustrated and to conclude that the efforts required in self-analysis are greater than the rewards obtained.

Explaining the Operation of the Media Equipment to Students

Unfamiliarity with media equipment can precipitate an unnatural or disruptive class reaction. In many classroom situations, media equipment represents the unknown. A simple procedure to acquaint students with the equipment is to exhibit and operate it for students prior to actual taping. Orientation to the media equipment often satisfies student curiosity. Familiarizing students with the equipment should lead to less abnormal behavior during the taping period.

A useful technique in minimizing the artificial atmosphere created by recording devices is to allow students to listen to or view themselves. This procedure will often satisfy undue student curiosity and allow for a more natural classroom reaction during taping sessions.

Explaining the Purpose of Teacher Self-Assessment to Students

A simple explanation of teacher self-assessment as well as a brief overview of the strategies involved in self-help is often an effective technique for allaying student fear and mistrust. Explaining the reason for and value of media equipment in self-assessment can help the teacher produce positive student attitudes and cooperation. Students usually perceive this activity as an act of honesty and forthrightness. As a consequence, student behavior becomes more natural during taping exercises.

Making Multiple Tapings to Minimize Unnatural Student Behavior

If unnatural student behavior in reaction to the presence of media equipment continues to be a problem, the teacher should tape the class several times or tape several different classes. In this fashion, the teacher can select the tape that is most representative of "normal" classroom interaction. It is important to remember that the teacher should seek to record typical interaction patterns rather than attempt to capture ideal teaching-learning interactions.

Knowing Where to Place the Microphone and Camera

Various methodological arrangements pose some difficult taping problems in teacher self-assessment. Small group instruction, independent study, and laboratory-oriented activities necessitate teacher behaviors that are different from those required for large-group lectures. The accurate placement of microphone and camera to capture these behaviors is essential. Loss of important interaction, garbled dialogue, or poor quality tapes will make it difficult for the teacher to carry out the other important steps in self-assessment.

Systematic and intelligent use of media equipment in self-assessment is vitally important. However, the use of media is only one of several strategies that can assist the teacher in comprehensive self-help practices. The use of media alone is an incomplete approach to self-help (Fuller and Manning, 1973)

STEP 3: IDENTIFYING BASIC TEACHING BEHAVIORS OF SET AND CLOSURE IN TEACHER SELF-ASSESSMENT

The use of audiotape or videotape recorder has been suggested as essential for gaining insight about teaching performance. However, the audiotape or videotape recorder can only provide the teacher with a limited amount of information.

The analysis of two basic skills—set and closure—can provide the teacher with a beginning framework for observing teaching performance. *Set* is defined as "those activities that are designed to prepare students for upcoming learning." *Closure,* the logical companion to set, is defined as "those activities designed to act as a capstone to learning that has occurred" (Bailey, 1980).

What Are the Essential Characteristics of Set?

In theory and practice, the purpose of set is to motivate students. Basic techniques to accomplish set include (1) stating goals or objectives of the lesson, (2) tying previous learning to upcoming learning, and (3) identifying procedures that will be utilized in upcoming learning activities. These simple techniques can help the teacher identify set when it occurs in the classroom performance; however, there are many questions that the teacher needs to consider when looking at set in the context of classroom teaching.

What Kind of Set Should Be Employed?

One of the basic questions that teachers must ask themselves when observing their set via audiotape or videotape is, Was the set that I used appropriate? Ultimately, the answer to that question depends on what the teacher was trying to accomplish. Therefore, the type of set observed (questions, review of objectives, etc.) should be closely allied to student intellectual, emotional, and physical needs, as well as to the desired educational outcomes.

A pattern of using two or three particular formats in set is commonly observed in teachers irrespective of instructional goals or student needs. Often, these routine patterns develop because the teacher becomes comfortable with the approach. Repetitive use of similar or identical sets, however, leads students to expect the same set over a period of time. Because predictable teacher behavior in the set often leads to student boredom, the teacher needs to question whether the set is motivating the students.

Although it is impossible to explore all alternative forms of set, it is important for teachers to be able to identify the kinds of sets they are currently using and sets they continue to use on a regular basis. The teacher who searches for alternative ways of establishing set will likely be the teacher finding the most effective methods for motivating students.

How Important Is Informal Set, or Preset?

Informal set, or *preset,* is defined as "the period of time in which students enter the classroom prior to formal instruction." It is that period of time in which students are finding their way to the classroom or those fleeting moments before the clock signals the beginning of class. Preset is a critical period of time for many students because it affects their subsequent attitudes toward and opinions expressed in the formal lesson.

The teacher's verbal and nonverbal cues during this period of time influence students to a great extent. Greeting students, laughing and talking with them, and establishing eye contact with them are all important teacher behaviors students observe prior to the class. Teacher behaviors observed in the preset period that can have a negative effect on students include irritability, silence, or physical absence. Environmental factors, such as room arrangement, lighting, and ventilation, also influence students in a conscious or unconscious manner. The various elements of preset help shape student attitudes and expectations that will ultimately develop in the formal set and instructional lesson.

What Are Negative and Positive Examples of Set?

Regrettably, the teacher will find it easier to identify negative examples of set than positive examples of set. Positive examples of set include those activities that involve students both mentally and physically. Examples include (1) asking questions that elicit student input, (2) making statements that reinforce the relevance of the concept being taught, (3) building upon previously taught concepts, and (4) establishing relationships between material currently being taught and what will be taught in the future. Often, a quality set involves a combination of all of these elements.

Negative examples of set include the following: (1) spending excessive time with clerical tasks (e.g., roll taking once class is scheduled to begin), (2) failing to indicate the importance and relevance of content under study, (3) speaking at great length to an individual student or group of students while the remaining class waits for class to begin, (4) failing to show the relationship between past learning and future learning, (5) habitually delaying classroom instruction by discussing personal interests or telling anecdotes or jokes, and (6) delaying classroom instruction by arranging the physical structure of the classroom for the planned instructional lesson.

Used on an infrequent basis, many of the activities described above are not totally ineffective. When these activities become representative teaching patterns, however, they suggest symptoms of unorganized or ineffective teaching. Attention to set by teachers in self-assessment practices will allow them to better understand the importance of motivating students.

How Often Does Set Occur?

Although the major set occurs at the beginning of class, set can and does occur many times during the instructional lesson. Any time the teacher initiates a new learning concept or activity or develops a new procedure, another form of set is needed. Other variables that affect the use of set are the particular student's needs, the age level of students, the concept being taught, and the length of the lesson.

Should Set Always Be Used?

Generally, set will always be required in the instructional lesson. Occasionally, however, set may be withheld or delayed. For example, the teacher may devise a learning activity and then follow that activity with a set that explains why the activity was performed. The initial withholding of set has the advantage of allowing the student to ponder the importance of the lesson being developed. However there should be definite reasons for withholding set. Set should never be withheld because of ignorance or lack of teacher planning.

How Much Time Should Be Devoted to Set?

The amount of time devoted to set will vary greatly from teacher to teacher. Set can occur in a few seconds, a few minutes, or even longer. Only the teacher can judge how much time is needed to prepare and motivate students for meaningful learning. The teacher can determine the length of set by asking the question, What do I need to do to prepare and motivate students to engage in this instructional lesson? Experimentation and careful analysis of recorded teaching lessons will be helpful in determining the exact amount of time needed for set establishment.

What Are the Essential Characteristics of Closure?

Closure, like set, can occur at any point in the classroom lesson. Closure is most frequently observed at the end of the instructional lesson, however, and includes assignments given by the teacher.

Closure is inherently more difficult than set. Many times the teacher deviates from the original lesson plan by developing student ideas as they unfold in class. As a consequence, the originally planned closure must be modified. This requires the teacher to summarize major accomplishments from memory, which tends to be more difficult than using the preplanned closure outline.

Possibly the greatest difficulty of closure is time management. The teacher must allow enough time for achieving closure. If the teacher has not managed time well in the instructional lesson, quality closure will be difficult or impossible to achieve. On occasion, teachers will let time run out or allow the bell to ring and not summarize the lesson. This is an example of closure by default. Lack of closure often leads to subsequent learning problems.

Closure should be planned and should include more than one type of activity. Summarizing, questioning, giving assignments, and projecting future activities are all activities that can be used in closure. Closure is a multifaceted function and an important part of the teaching-learning process.

How Important Are Students' Behaviors During Closure?

Verbal and nonverbal feedback from students during closure activities have a substantial effect on the teacher's performance. Intentionally or unintentionally, students manipulate teacher behavior through the use of positive and negative feedback. These positive and negative behaviors can be observed by watching students toward the end of the learning exercise or period. When students close their books, shuffle their feet, yawn, or continually check the clock, they are engaging in manipulative behavior; they are sending negative signals to the teacher. The effect of these signals on teacher behavior can result in premature or incomplete closure if the teacher is not aware of what is occurring. The teacher needs to be sensitive to student feedback during the closure period and should not allow students' behavior to negatively affect his or her attempts at closure.

Using student participation in closure can promote positive feedback from students. Allowing students to restate or identify important concepts that have been covered can facilitate successful closure.

What Are Long-Range Set and Long-Range Closure?

Long-range set is defined as "activities that prepare students for the upcoming semester or year." Setting the stage for learning is extremely important. Long-range set provides students with a structure for understanding the concepts and procedures that will be employed by the teacher. This activity provides an established set of boundaries for the student.

Long-range closure, or closure at the end of the course, is defined as "those activities that summarize learning that has occurred during the semester or year." Long-range closure can easily be overlooked by a teacher; however, closure at the end of the semester or year is equal in importance to long-range set. Restating learned concepts, summarizing learning in the context of the total course, and reviewing major questions that remain unanswered are vitally important activities because they allow the student to view what has occurred in relation to what will be occurring in the future. Long-range set and closure are necessary in providing continuity between subject matter found in a school curriculum.

The importance of set and closure has been underestimated in the past. There has been a tendency to believe that the actual lesson is more important than what happens at the beginning or end of the lesson. A teacher desiring to become proficient in teacher self-assessment practices will ultimately have to ask himself or herself the following questions:

- How aware am I of my set and closure?
- Am I using appropriate forms of set and closure?
- Am I using a variety of sets and closures?
- How can I improve my set and closure so that they result in a higher degree of student motivation?

STEP 4: IDENTIFYING VERBAL CUES IN TEACHER SELF-ASSESSMENT

One of the fundamental steps in teacher self-assessment is the identification of verbal behaviors. It is important for teachers to identify and analyze both verbal and nonverbal cues; however, it is critical for teachers to look at verbal cues individually before examining nonverbal cues.

At first glance, the identification of verbal behaviors is tremendously complex. However, researchers studying classroom interaction have devised systems for identifying those verbal behaviors that are common in teacher and student interaction (Lux and Bailey, 1972, Bailey and Lux, 1972). These systems can be used to analyze basic verbal instruction. Major areas of identification include (1) accepting and expressing emotions, (2) positive reinforcement, (3) feedback or building, (4) questioning, (5) information giving or lecturing, (6) direction giving, and (7) criticism or justifying authority. Teacher self-assessment requires that the teacher be able to identify each of these verbal behaviors on an in-depth basis.

Accepting/Expressing Emotions

Although expressing and/or accepting emotions is not as common as other types of teacher behaviors, it is an important verbal behavior. Accepting emotions may include clarifying or recalling past feelings shown by students. The following examples illustrate this verbal behavior:

- "I can understand how you feel."
- "Yesterday, many of us had the same feelings that you are expressing now."

The identification of this type of instructional behavior is important because it depicts a teacher who accepts and reacts to student feelings. Sometimes, teachers find the acceptance of students' emotions a difficult and uncomfortable activity. Dealing with subject matter is, at times, more easily accomplished than reacting to emotions shown by students.

Teachers need to recognize the importance of expressing their own feelings as well as accepting students' feelings. This type of behavior includes clarifying personal feelings and recalling past feelings. The following statements are examples of this type of verbal behavior:

- "I become very angry when I see teachers get involved in local politics."
- "My feelings about abortion are very strong."

Positive Reinforcement*

For the purposes of this discussion *positive reinforcement* is defined as "praise or encouragement of student behavior." There are many purposes for using this verbal cue, including: (1) recognizing students for their contributions, (2) building students' confidence, and (3) encouraging students' participation. Most positive reinforcement teacher behaviors have the end result of creating a more positive learning environment. Positive teacher reinforcement is shown in the following examples:

- "That's a good answer."
- "Super job, Fred!"
- "Yes, that is correct."
- "The class has done well in several areas, including . . . ."

In the first three examples, the teacher is reinforcing an individual's behavior. In the last example, the teacher is reinforcing the class's behavior. There is a difference between these two types of positive reinforcement, and teachers should be able to recognize these two forms of reinforcement in their own teaching.

The kind of positive reinforcement that is used is probably more important than the number of times that reinforcement is employed. Variety in positive reinforcement is important, since repetitious or cliché-type reinforcement becomes boring to students and soon loses meaning.

The amount of time that positive reinforcement behavior lasts is also worthy of teacher recognition. For many teachers, positive reinforcement behaviors only last a fraction of a second. Positive reinforcement can be expanded for more than a few seconds by using complete sentences as opposed to short phrases or one word responses. The following are examples of complete sentence reinforcement:

- "That is an excellent analysis of Thoreau's statement on life."
- "John, your fifth point in the essay was well put."

Another possible dimension of positive reinforcement is the use of humor. *Teacher humor* in the form of positive reinforcement is defined

---

* The author's discussion of reinforcement is not intended to provide an in-depth analysis of reinforcement found in learning theory texts. The author's discussion is limited and simplified for self-analysis purposes. A more exhaustive interpretation of reinforcement as it relates to learning theory can be found in Ernest R. Hilgard and Gordon H. Bower, *Theories of Learning*, 4th edition (Englewood Cliffs, N. J.: Prentice Hall, 1975) and in Wesley C. Becker, Siegfried Engelmann, and Don R. Thomas, *Instructor's Manual for Teaching: A Course in Applied Psychology* (Chicago: Science Research Associates, Inc., 1971).

as "a statement or a series of statements intended to relieve tension or amuse students." Sarcasm and ridicule are not included in this type of humor, since these behaviors have a tendency to threaten or embarrass students. The primary purpose of instructional humor is to relax the learning situation and assist in creating a positive learning atmosphere. The use of humor is shown in the following examples:

- "The concept of assassination will be covered today . . . . You should get a good bang out of this topic."
- "Please do not copy this diagram on the board. It has been *copyrighted* and is *protected* under the law."

Humor can assist the teacher in establishing a healthy learning environment and can increase attention and pupil interest; however, it should be noted that the relationship between humor and comprehension has not been proven. In fact, some studies reveal that humor related in classroom delivery may result in the student remembering the joke or humor rather than the content that was delivered or discussed (Kaplan and Pascoe, 1977).

Nonverbal behaviors are discussed under a separate heading; however, it is important to note here that nonverbal positive reinforcement can be an effective alternative to verbal reinforcement. Nonverbal positive reinforcement is teacher behavior that condones student behavior without overt verbal reinforcement. Nonverbal reinforcement can be manifested in many ways, such as facial expressions, travel, and hand gestures. The intended purpose of these nonverbal cues is the same as that of verbal positive reinforcement: to signal correct or appropriate behavior and encourage further participation. The following are examples of nonverbal positive reinforcement:

- A wink of an eye to indicate a correct response.
- Placing a hand on students' shoulders or backs to reassure them that they are proceeding correctly.
- Nodding the head to indicate a correct response.

The compulsion to use verbal reinforcement when a nonverbal response could be equally or more effective needs to be recognized by teachers. The nonverbal reinforcement cue is an excellent alternative behavior when verbal positive reinforcement has become repetitious or monotonous in classroom interaction.

Feedback or Building

Feedback or building is defined as "teacher statements that buttress, develop, or elaborate on the student's response." Teacher feedback is a vital behavior in classroom interaction. These verbal cues indicate the teacher's acceptance of or interest in the student's idea. Heavy use of feedback is characteristic of a learning environment in which ideas are being presented by both the student and the teacher. Building on student ideas also indicates that the teacher is flexible in his or her approach, since this act suggests that the teacher is willing to work with student ideas as they are presented.

Feedback or building is sometimes a difficult behavior because it requires the teacher to carefully listen to the student. Allowing enough time to listen to students' ideas is not always easy when the teacher has developed a lesson plan and a designated amount of material must be covered.

Feedback or building behavior becomes especially difficult if the teacher is bringing up an idea previously stated by a student. Feedback in this fashion demonstrates that the teacher is giving credit to the student for originating the idea, even though the idea was presented in a previous class session. Student reaction to this kind of teacher cue is usually positive because it signals that the teacher has recognized the quality of the student's idea. Heavy use of feedback techniques allows for and fosters greater interaction of students in the classroom. This type of feedback or building behavior is shown in the following examples:

- "As Tom stated, the thermostat control is always . . . ."
- "Let's develop that idea a bit more by saying . . . ."
- "As Mac said last week, it came into being because they were . . . ."

Another form of teacher feedback occurs when the teacher repeats or rephrases the student's response. Repeating the response or paraphrasing it is a method of accepting the content of the answer without providing immediate positive reinforcement. A second major purpose of this teacher behavior is to ensure that all students consider the idea voiced by the student. A third major purpose for this technique is to ensure that the student's response was audible to the rest of the class. A fourth purpose of this type of feedback is to encourage students to continue the discussion or signal students that the message was received.

Another feedback or building technique is the process of recognizing the student who desires to contribute to the classroom interaction. It is vitally important for the teacher to recognize students who wish to contribute. Such behavior communicates to students that the teacher is interested in them and desires to involve them in the classroom interaction. Under normal classroom conditions, a host of student verbal and nonverbal cues are sent to the teacher that signal the need to participate. Teachers who do not read these cues are likely to experience difficulty in controlling participation (i.e., some students will speak at will or some students will never speak). Students are generally appreciative of the teacher who recognizes their needs and desires as they relate to their classroom involvement. Examples of this type of behavior are as follows:

- "Pat, I noticed that you had your hand up a minute ago."
- "Ginny, you winced when I made that last statement; did you . . .?"

Questioning

There are several kinds of teacher questioning techniques as well as purposes for the use of questions. A teacher who desires to create maximum learning conditions should be keenly aware of the kinds of questions that are employed and the corresponding responses of students.

There are different categories of questions that can be employed that reflect intellectual difficulty or levels of thinking: (1) content-level questions, (2) analysis-level questions, and (3) decision-level questions. Other important types of questions are (1) feeling-level questions, (2) throwback questions, (3) structure or process questions, and (4) wait-time questions.

Content-Level Questions

Content-level questions may be defined as interrogative statements that require factual recall by the student. In addition, enumeration, labeling, or categorizing-type questions would come under the title of content-level questions. Some common functions of content-level questions are to test the student's knowledge of reading material and to establish a base of information upon which higher levels of cognitive thinking can take place. The following are examples of content-level questions:

- "What is the name of . . . ."

- "Who is the author of . . . ."
- "Name the five species in . . . ."
- "How many items belong under this title?"

Analysis-Level Questions

Analysis-level questions require students to analyze or explain information. The purpose of analysis-level questions is to get students to do more than recall factual information. Examples of analysis-level questions are the following:

- "What does this mean?"
- "Why did that happen?"
- "What would happen if . . .?"
- "Would you expand on that?"

Decision-Level Questions

Decision-level questions are interrogative statements that require the student to make a decision about content or procedure. The student's ability to make decisions is important. To facilitate this student behavior, the teacher needs to know how to frame questions to allow students to make decisions. The following are examples of this type of question:

- "How can we apply this . . .?"
- "Which alternative is best?"
- "Which laboratory exercise best fits the results of . . .?"
- "What should we do?"

Feeling-Level Questions

Feeling-level questions are interrogative statements that solicit students' feelings or attitudes. The purpose of asking this type of question is to encourage students to voice their feelings and to provide a chance for student involvement without risk of being right or wrong. Examples of feeling-level questions are the following:

- "Do you like . . .?"
- "What is your opinion of . . .?"
- "Personally, do you think you would . . . ?"

Throwback Questions

The throwback question is the act of referring a question back to the student or class. When a teacher turns a student's comment or question back to the student or class, it is considered a throwback technique. The purpose of a throwback question may differ according to the teacher's methodology. One of the major purposes of a throwback question is to allow the student to think about the question. This technique causes the student or class to reflect on the subject being discussed and arrive at answers for themselves rather than being dependent on the teacher for the answer. The following are examples of throwback questions:

- "What does the class think about Jack's question?"
- "Emmy, what do you think the answer is?"
- "Any reactions to that question?"

Students may resist the throwback question technique if they are accustomed to directive teachers. For a number of students, arriving at conclusions themselves without prior assistance from the teacher is difficult and uncomfortable. Therefore, the teacher needs to work with students to ensure that they know the teacher's motives for employing the throwback question.

Structure or Process Questions

An important, but often overlooked, questioning technique is the use of structure or process questions. Structure or process questions are questions that relate to procedures, including assignments or planned activities. Questions of this sort signal students that they may ask questions about what is going to occur or if they need clarification. This behavior affords students the opportunity to clarify nebulous ideas. Some examples of structure or process questions are the following:

- "Are there any questions about the assignment?"
- "Any further comments about . . . ?"
- "Does everyone understand what we are going to do today?"

Asking structure questions is a vital behavior if the teacher desires the majority of the class to conform to instructional expectations. If such questions are absent, students may not feel comfortable asking for clarification or may choose not to comply with teacher expectations.

Structure or process questions should be analyzed for their specificity. If the structure or process question is too general, the student may feel uncomfortable in responding to it. Therefore, the teacher needs to be able to formulate the question in such a way that the student can respond to it. Some examples of specific structure or process questions are the following:

- "Are there any questions about the 10 items covered on the topic of energy conservation?"
- "Does everyone understand what items should be brought to school tomorrow?"

Wait-Time Questions

The amount of time that elapses between the teacher's question and student's answer is called wait time or lag time. Researchers find that teachers are often unwilling to wait more than a fraction of a second when allowing students to answer questions (Rowe, 1974). Wait time of more than a second allows students to pause and reflect on questions posed by the teacher.

Teachers and students are sometimes uncomfortable with silence following questions. As a consequence, the teacher will rephrase the question or direct the question to another student before allowing the first student called on to answer the question. Teachers engaging in self-help activities will want to become aware of how long they wait for answers to their questions.

Silence lasting longer than a few seconds is less common and probably serves a purpose other than giving students a chance to think. Silence for long periods of time (5 seconds or longer) is more likely to be viewed as a control or discipline technique than as a constructive measure to allow the student to do in-depth thinking. Whether the purpose of silence is control or allowing students time to think, teachers need to be aware of how the silence is being interpreted by students.

Information Giving or Lecturing

Although information giving or lecturing has received less than favorable endorsements as a major methodology in the past, this expository style of teaching remains valuable. Lecturing is an efficient and effective way of communicating new information to students.

The giving of facts, explanations, analyses, and conclusions and the posing of rhetorical questions would be classified as lecturing. The purposes of lecturing are to introduce new material, to illustrate basic concepts, to focus attention on certain material, and to review material that has been covered previously. Examples of this type of verbal behavior are the following:

- "American clowns can be categorized into five groups. They are . . . ."
- "Why is alcoholism a danger? It is a danger because it has . . . ."
- "Today, we want to learn about adding two-digit numbers . . . ."

Lecturing with visual support is defined as "giving facts or opinions about content or procedures while simultaneously presenting visual stimuli." Information giving or lecturing for long periods of time requires an expanded student attention span. Handout sheets, chalkboard, transparencies on an overhead projector, and three-dimensional models are some of the more common examples of visual materials that can be used. Their basic value lies in enhancing the potential for message clarity. Examples of statements that refer to visual material include the following:

- "On this transparency you will see that each component is . . . ."
- "The handout illustrates that 54 percent of the insects . . . ."
- "This globe that I have in my hand indicates that the world is not round but oval . . . ."

Direction Giving

Direction giving is defined as "directions, commands, or orders with which a student is expected to comply." Direction giving as a verbal technique is important because both the teacher and the students must know the goal of the group and the means by which that goal will be achieved. Direction giving is also important if the teacher expects students to be ready to engage in subsequent learning activities. This verbal behavior is commonly observed in the following forms:

- "Your assignment for tomorrow is . . . ."
- "Fill out the paper according to the directions given."
- "For this activity, I want all of you to get in a circle."

Directions can be given with emphasis to stress main points or call attention to major concepts. Direction giving with emphasis enables the teacher to indicate what information is important.

Giving directions with emphasis as a verbal technique is also used to point out concepts that may have been missed by students and to keep students moving toward their goal. This verbal skill is especially effective as a measure for regaining the attention of the students.

Examples of directions given with emphasis are the following:

- "The first main point I want you to remember is . . . ."
- "Let me repeat that important idea so that you will . . . ."
- "Let me reemphasize the importance of this point by saying . . . ."

Criticism or Justifying Authority*

Criticism of a student or the total class is acceptable in classroom interaction. Criticism or negative reinforcement is used as an attempt to change unacceptable behavior patterns to acceptable behavior patterns or to justify or clarify the lines of authority.

Corrective verbal patterns vary from teacher to teacher and situation to situation. It is important for the teacher to be aware of when criticism is used, why it is used, and what the impact of the technique is on student behavior. Criticism can be used to redirect student interest and correct forms of inattention. Some examples of criticism are the following:

- "John, take your seat and be quiet!"
- "Most of the class failed the test. You had better start . . . ."
- "Don, that will be enough!"

---

* The author's discussion of criticism and negative reinforcement should not be viewed as a comprehensive analysis of negative reinforcement as it relates to learning theory. The author's explanations of criticism and negative reinforcement in this text are limited and simplistic for the purpose of self-analysis. A more exhaustive interpretation of negative reinforcement can be found in Ernest R. Hilgard and Gordon H. Bower, *Theories of Learning,* 4th edition (Englewood Cliffs, N. J.: Prentice Hall, 1975) and in Wesley C. Becker, Siegfried Engelmann, and Don R. Thomas, *Instructor's Manual for Teaching: A Course in Applied Psychology* (Chicago: Science Research Associates, Inc, 1971).

Negative reinforcement is also used by the teacher to convey that the student comment was incorrect or incomplete. The following are some examples of this type of negative reinforcement:

- "No, that is not correct."
- "Well, that is not quite what I had in mind."
- "That doesn't answer the question very well."

The analysis of verbal behaviors in self-assessment practices is an exciting exercise. The teacher who is serious about identifying what occurs in teacher-student interaction will find that there is a close relationship between teacher verbal behaviors and corresponding student verbal behaviors. The importance of verbal analysis activities lies in the recognition that teacher verbal behaviors fit together in a pattern. When a teacher studies these behaviors in a systematic fashion, he or she can learn to control them to maximize student learning. The selection of appropriate teacher verbal behaviors to produce desired student outcomes is not an idealistic instructional dream; it is the outcome of prudent use of self-assessment practices.

STEP 5: IDENTIFYING NONVERBAL CUES IN TEACHER SELF-ASSESSMENT

Teachers engaging in self-assessment will find that the identification and study of nonverbal behavior involves some unique and awesome problems. There are literally thousands of random nonverbal behaviors that can be observed. (See Miller, 1981.)

The following discussion focuses on the 10 major nonverbal cues used most often by teachers in the classroom: (1) eye contact, (2) gestures, (3) mannerisms, (4) travel, (5) touching, (6) facial expressions, (7) posture, (8) energy level, (9) use of space, and (10) silence.

Eye Contact

Eye contact ranks high in importance among the nonverbal behaviors found in a teacher's total repertoire. How eye contact is interpreted by the student depends on the purpose of this nonverbal cue and how the cue is delivered in the context of the instructional lesson.

There are four major purposes for the use of eye contact:

- *approval:* looking into a student's eyes in a condoning fashion when acceptable verbal or physical behavior is observed.

- *interest:* gazing into a student's eyes to communicate acceptance of the student's behavior and teacher sincerity.
- *disapproval or control:* staring at a student or looking into a student's eyes to indicate disapproval or to change unacceptable behavior to acceptable behavior.
- *listening:* looking into a student's eyes to indicate that his or her message is being received and understood.

Eye contact is a critical skill because students are continually measuring whether congruity exists between what is being said verbally and what is being communicated with the eyes. If the teacher is sending one message verbally but communicating the opposite message with eye contact, students will recognize the conflict. When a conflict occurs, the nonverbal behavior overrides the verbal signal. Failure to indicate the same message verbally and with eye contact can make the teacher appear insincere or hypocritical to the student.

Another major reason for identifying and studying eye contact as a nonverbal cue is that teachers need to recognize when eye contact as a nonverbal cue would be more effective than verbal behavior. Teachers need to view eye contact as an alternative behavior to sending the verbal message.

In addition to knowing how and when to use eye contact, teachers must be aware of whom they are looking at when they employ eye contact as an instructional technique. With the aid of the audiotape or videotape recorder, teachers can determine whether they look at some students in the classroom more than others. Teacher eye contact is usually established with students who send positive eye signals rather than with students who fail to establish eye contact or send neutral eye contact messages. Other reasons why a teacher establishes regular eye contact with a particular student include (1) the student answers questions or interacts on a regular basis, (2) the student is a discipline problem, and (3) the student attempts to draw attention to himself or herself through verbal or nonverbal manipulation. While there are several reasons for establishing eye contact, it is important for the teacher to study systematically the eye contact techniques he or she employs for both awareness and control.

Gestures

Gestures are those nonverbal behaviors teachers have incorporated into their teaching. Gestures are significant because they buttress the verbal message being sent by the teacher. Gestures also communicate the degree of emotion that the teacher attaches to the verbal message. Strong feelings are usually accompanied by very specific gestures.

For some teachers, gestures are a way of acting out physically what they are attempting to communicate verbally. In many instances, gesturing can be used to help the student understand the verbal message when it is blurred or unintelligible.

Teachers may not be aware of their gestures or try to control them. Any portion of the teacher's body can be used for gesturing: legs, feet, head, shoulders, trunk, or hands. Use of the hands is the most commonly observed gesture.

Mannerisms

A mannerism can be classified as a nonverbal companion behavior to a gesture. All portions of the body that are used in gestures can also be used in mannerisms: head, hands, shoulders, trunk, legs, or feet. However, the most common instructional mannerisms are teacher hand and head movements. Mannerisms and gestures are often confused by the novice observer in self-assessment. Mannerisms are usually mindless behaviors (they occur without instructional purpose or reason) that have little or no relationship to what is being said or done by the teacher. Simply stated, mannerisms are examples of idiosyncratic behavior.

Teacher mannerisms are fairly easy to identify. Scratching the face, wrinkling the nose, tugging at clothing, playing with eyeglasses, and tapping the fingers are all illustrations of mannerisms. Mannerisms can be both positive and negative in nature. Some mannerisms make teachers unique and endear them to students; other mannerisms can be annoying, distracting, and even damaging to the teaching process.

Mannerisms appear and disappear in a teacher's behavior in an erratic fashion. Some mannerisms appear and remain for a long period of time; other mannerisms are retained for a short period of time. Mannerisms are often prompted by a physical need. For example, the need to scratch the nose can lead to repeated scratching of the nose. The teacher who has been standing for several hours will begin to shift from one foot to the other. Soon the shifting of the weight from one foot to the other becomes a repetitive, meaningless behavior. When this occurs, the behavior can be classified as a mannerism.

The physical availability of objects can permit or foster the development of a mannerism. For example, a teacher who has facial hair (mustache or beard) may stroke it on a regular basis. Another example of a mannerism is the jingling of coins found in the pocket. The coin-jingling mannerism often forces students to focus on the noise rather than on what is being said by the teacher. Teachers who wish to prevent this type of mannerism can simply remove the object or make it difficult to touch during the class period. Recognizing the potential hazard of objects in mannerism development is critical to a teacher's instructional control of nonverbal cues.

Detection of both positive and negative teaching mannerisms is not always easy in self-assessment activities. The use of a videotape recorder can be an efficient way of identifying both positive and negative mannerisms. Students' immediate verbal or nonverbal reactions to teaching behavior will often indicate acceptable or unacceptable mannerisms. However, identification of nonverbal mannerisms that are helpful, neutral, or distracting is sometimes best accomplished by soliciting feedback from students (Bailey, 1978).

Travel

The teacher's physical movement in the classroom is a powerful nonverbal behavior. Nonverbal messages are conveyed to students when the teacher (1) travels to certain areas in the classroom, (2) travels at different times in the period or day, (3) travels at different speeds, and (4) travels to certain individuals in the room.

Traveling can have a definite purpose, or it can be a mindless behavior. When teacher travel becomes a mindless behavior, it is classified as a mannerism. Pacing back and forth in front of the class during a lecture can be labeled a mannerism.

Teacher travel can and should have purpose in the classroom. Travel can be used for the following purposes:

- *reinforcement:* traveling over to a student to indicate that his or her behavior or performance is acceptable.
- *availability:* moving next to a student to indicate a willingness to answer questions or provide assistance.
- *control or discipline:* walking toward inappropriate student activities to control behavior.

Teachers establish regular travel paths in a classroom. Established routine and familiarity with particular students are common explanations for frequently traveled areas. The methodology being used, control, and rapport with students are also important variables affecting teacher travel.

One of the most significant variables influencing teacher travel appears to be the personal security of the teacher. Teachers generally travel to students and areas of the room where they feel comfortable or have established control. Comfort or feeling free to travel is directly linked to personal relationships with students. The teacher is much more likely to travel to students who are warm and responsive and is less likely to travel to cool, unresponsive, or belligerent students.

The traffic pattern established by the teacher can also be influenced by the structure of the classroom. The room style and furniture arrangement can dictate traffic patterns. Room arrangement affects where the teacher will travel as well as where the teacher wants students to travel. Therefore, the teacher should take great care in arranging furniture in the classroom to facilitate or hamper travel.

Touching

Touching represents one of the paradoxes found in our society. Touching children in the home by family members is not uncommon and usually acceptable. Touching among players and between coach and players is widely accepted in football, basketball, and other sports. However, touching in the classroom by the teacher is subject to a different interpretation.

Although touching is one of the more controversial nonverbal cues in a teacher's repertoire, it remains one of the most significant teaching tools in the teacher's instructional performance. Unfortunately, not much is known about the effects of touching in elementary and secondary school settings. Even less is known about how touching affects the adult learner. Many elementary teachers endorse the concept of touching, whereas teachers in the upper grades (junior high, high school, and college) are more cautious about touching students.

Regardless of the personal bias of the teacher, touching has many uses in the classroom:

- *reinforcement:* touching or making physical contact with a student to show approval.
- *control or discipline:* touching or making physical contact with a student to show disapproval or to change unacceptable behavior to acceptable behavior. Extreme forms of physical contact, such as spanking, hitting, or paddling, are included in this category.

- *reassurance:* touching a student to indicate interest, sincerity, understanding, or concern.

Age level, student maturity, instructional context of the touch, sex of the teacher, and sex of the student are all variables teachers should consider when touching in the classroom. A teacher studying personal instructional touching habits needs to ask himself or herself the following questions:

- Do I touch?
- When do I touch?
- Whom do I touch?
- How often do I touch?
- Why do I touch?
- Can my touching be interpreted in the wrong way by students? teachers? parents? administrators?

In addition to considering the above questions, the teacher needs to be very conscious of the manner in which a student responds to touching. Some students are extremely receptive to touching; others have mild or even violent objections to being touched. The manner in which a student responds to touching has to be foremost in the mind of the teacher. The teacher can determine whether a student responds favorably to touching by observing the student over a period of time and recognizing the specific needs of that student.

Situations and circumstances dictate when, where, and whom the teacher can touch. Invasion of personal rights and explicit or implicit sexual overtones must be avoided. While common sense must be exercised in any instructional situation, touching remains one of the most powerful forms of nonverbal communication known in teaching.

Facial Expressions

Certain nonverbal cues are so interlaced with the total verbal makeup of teachers that it is sometimes difficult to study them in isolation. Facial expressions fall into this category. Excluding the eye area (which was discussed under "Eye Contact"), there are eight major areas of the teacher's face that can communicate messages: (1) forehead, (2) eyebrows, (3) cheeks, (4) nose, (5) ears, (6) lips, (7) tongue, and (8) chin.

When a message is sent by the teacher verbally, a portion of the facial region is also involved. The student compares what the teacher is saying verbally with what the teacher's face is communicating nonverbally. Achieving congruity between what is being said and how it is being said facially is extremely important, especially if the teacher wishes to establish credibility with students.

Individually, certain facial expressions may not appear to be powerful. Collectively, they can communicate some significant messages: surprise, disapproval, affection, or sincerity. Effective teachers recognize the potential of their facial features and use them to their advantage in communicating effectively and efficiently.

No other portion of the body communicates as many different messages as the face does. Unfortunately, the teacher can convey messages facially unwillingly or unknowingly. The following questions can be used to assist the teacher in becoming more aware of how his or her facial expressions influence instruction:

- What kind of image do my facial expressions reflect?
- Are my facial expressions congruent with what I am saying verbally?
- How can I control my facial features to assist in achieving the objectives for the lesson?
- What nonverbal facial messages can be used in lieu of overused or common verbal messages?

Posture

The manner in which teachers position themselves in the classroom is extremely significant. Whether the teacher stands, sits, slouches, or stoops, the posture influences the learner. In self-assessment practices, it is impossible to generalize that there is one right way of posturing. However, it is important for the teacher to become aware of the different messages conveyed with posture.

Major messages conveyed by posture include warmth, sincerity, and interest on the part of the teacher. Posture also communicates a teacher's expectations of students. A relaxed posture can communicate an informal learning activity, whereas a formal or rigid posture can communicate a more work-oriented or task-oriented activity. The teacher can create a different kind of instructional image with a different form of posture. In self-assessment, the teacher needs to determine how this posture affects students' attitudes and performance. Teachers must learn to view their posture in an objective fashion. To do this, four major questions should be considered:

- What kind of posture do I use in the classroom?
- Is my posture consistent with the methods that I am using?
- Can I use another form of posture to bring about more effective, efficient learning in students?
- What messages are being communicated with my posture?

Energy Level

Energy level is one of the more elusive nonverbal behaviors for teachers engaged in self-help activities. A teacher's energy level can be readily observed, but individual characteristics of that energy level are difficult to discuss because so many verbal and nonverbal behaviors are involved.

Awareness of teacher energy level and its effects on student performance is important in self-assessment practices. Teachers will find that energy level is analogous to a barometer, which fluctuates from high to low and low to high. Energy-level fluctuations will occur during the day, week, month, and year.

Teachers can easily chart changes in their energy level to determine when and why there is a variation by keeping an energy-level diary. By recording the variations, teachers can learn more about energy level and how to control this nonverbal cue instead of allowing it to control them.

There is no ideal energy level in teaching. Teachers need to recognize, however, that the energy level of students can be raised or lowered by raising or lowering the instructional energy level. For example, a teacher can control a class that exhibits a great deal of excitement and enthusiasm by demonstrating a moderate energy level. Conversely, a teacher who exhibits a dynamic, exciting energy level can raise the energy level of a class that is rather sedate and unexcited.

It is imperative for teachers to learn how to control personal teaching energy level before attempting to modify or influence student energy level. A primary task of teachers is to determine the nature of personal energy level so that they can exhibit an energy level that has the most positive effect on students' learning and performance.

Use of Space

The nonverbal message delivered by classroom arrangement can be substantial. The way that a teacher arranges or organizes the classroom affects how the students will act when they enter the room. Classroom arrangement denotes the activities planned and the teacher's expectations of students during the period. As discussed earlier, the arrangement of the classroom also affects the teacher's ability to travel in the classroom.

A nonverbal message is communicated to students by designating areas for students' use and areas used by the teacher. The diagram in Figure 3 denotes specific areas that are used for a given activity in an elementary, junior high, or high school room. For the student, the area becomes associated with the instructional activity that will take place.

Figure 3
UTILIZATION OF SPACE IN THE CLASSROOM

<table>
<tr><td rowspan="3">Non-Use</td><td colspan="2">Independent Study</td><td rowspan="3">Play Area or Free Time</td></tr>
<tr><td colspan="2">Work or Study Area</td></tr>
<tr><td>Laboratory</td><td>Reading Area</td></tr>
</table>

The classroom illustration in Figure 3 also indicates potential areas that the teacher can establish for different instructional activities. If the teacher wants students to take advantage of a designated area, the visual arrangement of that area must communicate this message. Consequently, independent study areas should be made to look like independent study areas, and reading areas should have books and equipment needed for reading.

Obviously, there are some significant variables that affect how the teacher uses space in the classroom: age level of students, subject matter, actual classroom size, and methodology employed by the teacher. These variables must be weighed carefully when planning how to use the available space in the classroom.

Silence

Silence is one of the least obvious nonverbal cues in the teacher's nonverbal repertoire; however, it is one of the most important cues to master in nonverbal communication. Stage, television, radio, and motion picture personalities have always been renowned for their mastery of silence. Messages of overstatement and understatement, auras of suspense, and humor are all sent through the medium of silence.

In addition to wait-time questions (discussed earlier), there are many important uses of silence in the classroom that need to be explored. Silence in the form of a pause can be used to provoke thought in teacher-student interaction. In addition, a pause can be used by the teacher any time that higher levels of thought are required in the instruction.

Silence can be used as a method to increase the attention span of the listener. Unbroken speech patterns exhibited by the teacher can become very monotonous and boring to students. Carefully timed silence provides a break in the interaction, which allows the student to comprehend what has been said and to prepare for upcoming learning. On the other hand, ill-timed silence has the potential to become distracting to the listener. Thus, silence in the form of a pause must be carefully planned by the teacher.

Silence can also be used to control or discipline students. When unacceptable behavior occurs, the teacher can simply stop instruction and allow silence to occur, which denotes disapproval. The technique of silence as a control maneuver has been vastly underestimated in importance. Obviously, silence is usually accompanied by other nonverbal behaviors, such as facial disapproval and negative eye contact. The teacher will find that nonverbal control through silence can often be used as a substitute behavior for the more common verbal reprimand.

In self-assessment, it is important to remember that silence can be either positive or negative depending on how the teacher desires to use the behavior. Equally important, teachers must learn to feel comfortable with silence rather than fear it. Silence, like all other nonverbal behaviors, can be controlled and used to achieve positive student outcomes.

As experience and knowledge grow in the area of nonverbal communication, it is important to remember that there is no set of nonverbal behaviors that can be prescribed for effective teaching. Research and individual teacher study of nonverbal communication remain in an embryonic stage. With experience in self-assessment, the teacher will find the study of nonverbal behaviors an exciting and rewarding exercise.

STEP 6: PLANNING INSTRUCTIONAL BEHAVIORS WITH MEANS-REFERENCED OBJECTIVES

Thus far, self-assessment has been defined as a series of steps: (1) understanding what is involved in self-assessment, (2) using media to study the teaching self, (3) identifying basic skills of set and closure, (4) identifying verbal behaviors, and (5) identifying nonverbal behaviors. The next step in self-help activities is to learn how to plan and evaluate the instructional behaviors that the teacher has identified. Through the use of means-referenced objectives, the teacher can learn to control the specific methods that are used in the teaching act.

What Are Means-Referenced Objectives?

Means-referenced objectives (MROs) are statements that specify the exact method or means to be employed by the teacher to achieve an instructional end. MROs are written for one purpose: the improvement of instruction. The use of MROs provides teachers with an opportunity to expand ways of determining effectiveness by looking at the skills or methods that are used to bring about student learning.

What Is the Difference Between MROs and Instructional Objectives?

Means-referenced objectives and instructional objectives are equally important but distinctly different.* Instructional objectives have the potential to serve many valuable functions in helping teachers plan and organize student outcomes. However, they are limited in that they minimize the teacher's ability to focus on exact methods needed to achieve instructional ends. MROs were created with the purpose of filling the void inherent in instructional objectives. They are not intended to replace instructional objectives; they are companion statements that can be used with instructional objectives. For all practical purposes, teachers engaging in self-assessment practices would use both MROs and instructional objectives. However, it is conceivable that the teacher may desire to concentrate exclusively on important methods and therefore write only MROs.

* For a complete discussion of instructional objectives, see Robert F. Mager, *Preparing Instructional Objectives* (Belmont, Calif.: Fearon Publishing Co., 1962).

The similarities and differences between instructional objectives and MROs can be illustrated in the following manner:

Means-Referenced Objectives	*Instructional Objectives*
Written instruction of teacher outcomes (methodology).	Written instructions of student outcomes (achievement).
Written with three essential components: (1) condition(s), (2) type of activity, and (3) criteria for assessing the teacher's behavior.	Written with three essential components: (1) condition(s), (2) type of activity, and (3) criteria for assessing the student's behavior.
Related directly to the means (process or strategy) employed by the teacher to achieve instructional ends.	Related directly to the intended outcomes or student terminal behavior.
May or may not relate to three domains: cognitive, affective, and psychomotor.	Written in three domains: cognitive, affective, and psychomotor.

What Is the Purpose of MROs?

The purpose of writing MROs is to help teachers examine and improve the teaching process. Teachers will find MROs valuable in the three critical stages of teaching: (1) planning the instructional lesson, (2) conducting the instructional lesson, and (3) evaluating student performance.

The advantages of planning the instructional lesson are obvious. The teacher can determine which instructional strategy will assist the student in achieving preplanned outcomes. Equally important, the teacher is able to set a proficiency level (in terms of personal teaching performance) that is deemed as effective or acceptable. During the planning stage, the teacher is able to concentrate on possible alternative strategies that could be used to teach the same concept.

During the second stage of teaching, conducting the instructional lesson, the teacher can utilize MROs with the audiotape or videotape recorder. While listening to or viewing the teaching performance on tape, the teacher can use MROs to determine if the predetermined teaching behaviors were utilized. Variation between the written MROs and actual teaching behavior can provide insight about how to modify subsequent planned teaching behavior.

During the third stage of instruction, evaluating student performance, the performance measures in MROs can be used to pinpoint the exact methods used to teach the concept. This information allows the teacher to construct the most appropriate test items in relation to how the concepts were taught. After the test is completed, the teacher can assess student outcomes (performance) in relation to the strategy employed to reach the desired student outcome. The resulting information should suggest different or additional strategies that need to be employed to increase student achievement or attitude level.

What Is the Value of MROs?

The use of MROs allows teachers to chart professional growth patterns. In the process of self-assessment, MROs permit teachers to more accurately determine when they have reached established objectives.

MROs can also help teachers increase the flexibility of their instructional methods. One of the greatest potentials for MROs is their ability to assist the teacher in experimenting with and acquiring new skills.

The use of MROs can prevent or decrease the occurrence of inaccurate self-perceptions of teaching behavior. Previous research (Bailey, 1972) has indicated that teachers' self-perceptions differ from their actual classroom performance. Using MROs in self-assessment is a way for teachers to gather data on actual classroom performance to confirm or negate their opinions of how they perform in the classroom.

The use of MROs also enables teachers to look at themselves without focusing directly on student behavior. Looking at student behavior is important; however, MROs allow the teacher to focus exclusively on teacher behavior.

How Are MROs Written?

An MRO can be written for any teaching skill, technique, or strategy the teacher wishes to study or improve. MROs can be developed for any of the skills discussed under verbal and nonverbal cue identification. The following illustrates how MROs can be written.

Basic Verbal Cue	*Means-Referenced Objective*
Questioning	In a small group inquiry lesson on population explosion, the teacher will ask more analysis-level questions than content-level questions. Three out of four questions framed will be analysis-level questions.
Reinforcement	In a contracting exercise, the teacher will reinforce the student by using both single-word and complete-sentence reinforcement techniques. A minimum of two different single-word reinforcement behaviors and two different sentence behaviors will be utilized in the 10-minute session.

Basic Nonverbal Cue	*Means-Referenced Objective*
Eye Contact	During the 20-minute laboratory demonstration on mixing chemicals, the teacher will establish eye contact with 90 percent of the class. Criterion: 18 out of the 20 people will establish eye contact with the instructor for at least 1 second.
Travel	During the 10-minute work assignment in mathematics, the teacher will travel to each student. Criterion: 15 out of 15 students will have been contacted by the instructor to determine if further assistance is necessary.

How Are the "Means" in the MROs Determined?

The previous examples of MROs were associated with basic verbal and nonverbal cues that can be used on a daily basis. MROs need not be used exclusively for specific verbal and nonverbal cues. MROs can be developed for behaviors the teacher wishes to identify and evaluate on a long-term basis. Some examples of MROs that can be used for long-term self-improvement follow.

Behavior	*Means-Referenced Objective*
Respect and Self-Concept	In an attempt to model respect and concern for individuals, the teacher will verbally call on each child by name. Acceptable performance will be determined when the teacher accomplishes this task by the end of the first week of class.

Behavior	*Means-Referenced Objective*
Professional Self-Development	In an attempt to keep abreast of teacher research, the instructor will read professional magazines. Criterion: A minimum of four different magazines will be read in a 9-month period.

What Are the Essential Elements of an MRO?

An MRO consists of three elements: (1) condition: the condition under which the behavior is to be demonstrated, (2) type of activity: the nature of the behavior or attitude that is to be demonstrated, and (3) criteria: the standards or professional level to be applied in assessing the behavior. All three elements deal with the teaching method or strategy, and they are equally important.

Of the three elements of MROs, the criterion statement appears to give teachers the most difficulty when writing MROs. The criterion or standard will generally be an arbitrary statement. The subsequent analysis, showing achievement or lack of achievement of the criterion, provides insight into progress being made in self-improvement activities.

What Steps Are Used to Implement MROs in Self-Assessment?

The following steps illustrate how MROs can be used to improve self-assessment.

Step 1: Teacher identifies concepts that are to be taught and basic methods to be used in teaching the lesson.

Step 2: Teacher constructs lesson plan with aid of means-referenced objectives as a planning method.

Step 3: Teacher conducts lesson while audiotaping or videotaping performance.

Step 4: Teacher evaluates instructional methods using means-referenced objectives.

The use of MROs can be a valuable device in teacher self-assessment. MROs serve many different functions in planning, conducting, and evaluating the classroom lesson. The use of MROs not only allows the teacher to select critical teaching skills, but allows the teacher to learn how to control instructional behaviors.

STEP 7: USING OBSERVATION FORMS IN TEACHER SELF-ASSESSMENT

The ability to successfully engage in self-improvement requires several strategies. The development and use of observation instruments as a method for identifying and controlling instructional behavior is one of the most important steps in self-assessment. An observation instrument is a device employed by the teacher to identify classroom events captured by the audiotape or videotape recorder. Observation instruments are checklists that preserve specific behaviors, frequency of behaviors, and sequence of behaviors.

Selection of an observation instrument for self-assessment is not an easy task, since the choice can be made from over 100 different observation systems (Rosenshine and Furst, 1973; pp. 122–83). Some instruments deal specifically with verbal behaviors; a few instruments capture nonverbal behaviors. In addition, observation instruments can focus directly on teacher behavior or exclusively on student behavior. The degree of complexity of observation instruments varies. Some instruments record 1 or 2 behaviors, whereas others have the capacity to record 50 or more teacher or student behaviors.

There are two basic types of observation instruments available to the teacher engaging in self-help: expert-prepared instruments and teacher-made instruments. Expert-prepared instruments are those that have been developed by professionals in the field of observation instruments. Teacher-made observation instruments are those prepared by teachers who are involved in self-assessment practices. The purpose of preparing self-constructed instruments is to design materials specific to the individual needs of the teacher. Both the expert-prepared and the teacher-prepared observation instruments have value to the teacher engaging in self-help.

Expert-Prepared Observation Instruments

An example of an expert-prepared instrument most teachers are familiar with is Flanders' Interaction Analysis Categories (FIAC). Flanders' system of Interaction Analysis (Flanders, 1970) is illustrated in Figure 4. The system comprises 10 basic categories: (1) accepting feelings, (2) praising or encouraging, (3) accepting ideas, (4) asking questions, (5) lecturing, (6) giving directions, (7) criticizing or justifying authority, (8) student responding to teacher, (9) student-initiated talk, and (10) silence or confusion.

The Flanders instrument is concerned with verbal behavior and is recorded by the teacher every 3 seconds or whenever a different behavior occurs. Basically, the data gathered with the instrument classify teacher behavior that maximizes (indirect) or minimizes (direct) freedom of the student to respond. The classification system gives central attention to the amount of freedom a teacher gives to the student.

For many teachers engaging in self-assessment, expert-prepared systems, such as the FIAC, will be very appropriate. The use of Flanders' observation system represents an effective means for providing objective information. The subsequent analysis of these behaviors via matrix analysis and sequence graphs (Urback, 1966) provides a wealth of information to the teacher about personal instructional behavior.

A number of expert-prepared instruments provide the information needed for self-examination; however, some of these expert-prepared observation systems reveal shortcomings:

- A *substantial* number of these expert-prepared instruments focus only on verbal or nonverbal behaviors; only a few capture both verbal and nonverbal behaviors.
- Expert-prepared instruments are usually designed for either teacher-centered or teacher-controlled classrooms; rarely do they accommodate both types of classrooms. Teachers employ several student-centered methodologies. As a consequence, a number of expert-prepared instruments are not usable because they do not capture student-centered activities.
- A number of expert-prepared observation instruments are difficult to master by the teacher. Training, coding, and subsequent data analysis can involve several hours.

Teacher-Made Observation Instruments

The alternative to expert-prepared observation instruments is teacher-made observation forms. The actual scoring of these instruments takes place during an audiotape or videotape playback session. With a minimum of training and information, teachers can create observation forms that suit their particular instructional situations. Measures of reliability and validity are difficult to obtain with these instruments; how-

Figure 4
FLANDERS' INTERACTION ANALYSIS CATEGORIES* (FIAC)

Teacher Talk	Response	1. *Accepts feeling.* Accepts and clarifies an attitude or the feeling tone of a pupil in a nonthreatening manner. Feelings may be positive or negative. Predicting and recalling feelings are included. 2. *Praises or encourages.* Praises or encourages pupil action or behavior. Jokes that release tension, but not at the expense of another individual; nodding head, or saying "Um hm?" or "go on" are included. 3. *Accepts or uses ideas of pupils.* Clarifying, building, or developing ideas suggested by a pupil. Teacher extensions of pupil ideas are included but as the teacher brings more of his own ideas into play, shift to category five.
		4. *Asks questions.* Asking a question about content or procedure, based on teacher ideas, with the intent that a pupil will answer.
	Initiation	5. *Lecturing.* Giving facts or opinions about content or procedures; expressing *his own* ideas, viving *his own* explanation, or citing an authority other than a pupil. 6. *Giving directions.* Directions, commands, or orders to which a pupil is expected to comply. 7. *Criticizing or justifying authority.* Statements intended to change pupil behavior from nonacceptable to acceptable pattern; bawling someone out; stating why the teacher is doing what he is doing; extreme self-reference.
Pupil Talk	Response	8. *Pupil-talk—response.* Talk by pupils in response to teacher. Teacher initiates the contact or solicits pupil statement or structures the situation. Freedom to express own ideas is limited.
	Initiation	9. *Pupil-talk—initiation.* Talk by pupils which they initiate. Expressing own ideas; initiating a new topic; freedom to develop opinions and a line of thought, like asking thoughtful questions; going beyond the existing structure.
Silence		10. *Silence or confusion.* Pauses, short periods of silence and periods of confusion in which communication cannot be understood by the observer.

* There is *no* scale implied by these numbers. Each number is classificatory; it designates a particular kind of communication event. To write these numbers down during observation is to enumerate, not to judge a position on a scale.

SOURCE: Flanders, *Analyzing Teaching Behavior,* © 1970, Addison-Wesley Publishing Company, Inc., chapter 2, page 34, Table 2-1, "Flanders' Interaction Analysis Categories (FIAC)." Reprinted with permission.

ever, they offer several advantages for self-assessment practices:

- Teachers can create observation instruments that capture the specific skills they are most interested in. Instruments can be tailored to capture interaction information for either teacher-centered or student-centered classrooms.
- A self-made observation form can be designed to study both verbal and nonverbal behaviors.
- A self-made observation instrument can be a comprehensive form that enables the teacher to look at multiple behaviors rather than a select few.
- The self-made observation form can provide the teacher with a process for examining both verbal and nonverbal behaviors on an in-depth basis. This in-depth analysis activity leads the teacher to a better understanding of the teaching and learning acts.
- The self-made observation form requires an investment of creative activity in terms of teacher time. This type of investment fosters a need for continued use of the instrument, which leads to long-term self-assessment activities.

Self-made observation instruments are not without limitations. The shortcomings of these instruments should be weighed against the advantages of expert-prepared instruments:

- The process of creating observation instruments can be time-consuming.
- Self-made observation instruments seldom lend themselves to reliability and validity measurement as do expert-prepared observation instruments.
- A self-made observation instrument often reflects the bias of its creator.

The creation of self-made observation forms necessitates the examination of three major behavior facets. Although not all instruments will capture all three, the following facets should be carefully considered by the teacher when creating observation forms: (1) identification of instructional behaviors (what behavior is observed), (2) frequency of behaviors (how often the behavior occurs), and (3) sequence of behaviors (in what order behaviors occur).

Identification of Behaviors

The first step in creating a self-made observation form is to determine which behaviors are to be observed. In this activity, the teacher must carefully consider which behaviors are important to observe. Both verbal and nonverbal behaviors or other basic teaching skills (i.e., set and closure) can be identified. The teacher will also need to determine how many of these verbal and nonverbal behaviors will need to be observed.

Frequency of Behaviors

Recording frequency of behaviors requires the teacher to consider how often a behavior is occurring in the classroom interaction. For example, if the teacher is interested in observing both verbal and nonverbal behaviors, the instrument will have to be designed to capture the number of times specific behaviors are repeated. Figure 5 is an example of a frequency observation form designed for that purpose.

Figure 5
FREQUENCY OBSERVATION FORM DEALING WITH SELECTED VERBAL AND NONVERBAL BEHAVIORS

Directions: Place a tally mark after each behavior when it occurs in the designated 3-minute interval.

	3 minutes	6 minutes	9 minutes	12 minutes	15 minutes
Travel					
—reinforcement					
—availability					
—control					
Eye Contact					
—approval					
—interest					
—disapproval					
—listening					
Positive Reinforcement					
—single word					
—sentence					
—humor					
—individual student .					
—class					

Sequence of Behaviors

Recording a sequence of behaviors with a self-made observation instrument can be a complicated process. The teacher must determine the sequence of behaviors. The frequency of both verbal and nonverbal behaviors can be identified, or the observation instrument can be designed to focus on one behavior exclusively. This observation feature usually requires considerable forethought.

The form in Figure 6 depicts how one behavior can be observed with sequence as the major consideration. The observation form records the sequence of content-level, analysis-level, decision-level, and wait-time questions.

Figure 6
SEQUENCE OBSERVATION FORM DEALING WITH TYPES OF QUESTIONS

Directions: Use the following symbols to record the type of question observed.

C Content-level question
A Analysis-level question
D Decision-level question
W Wait-time question

Record the type of question when it occurs in the recording columns. Record only the questions asked of students. Begin with the first column. At the end of each minute, shift to the next column.

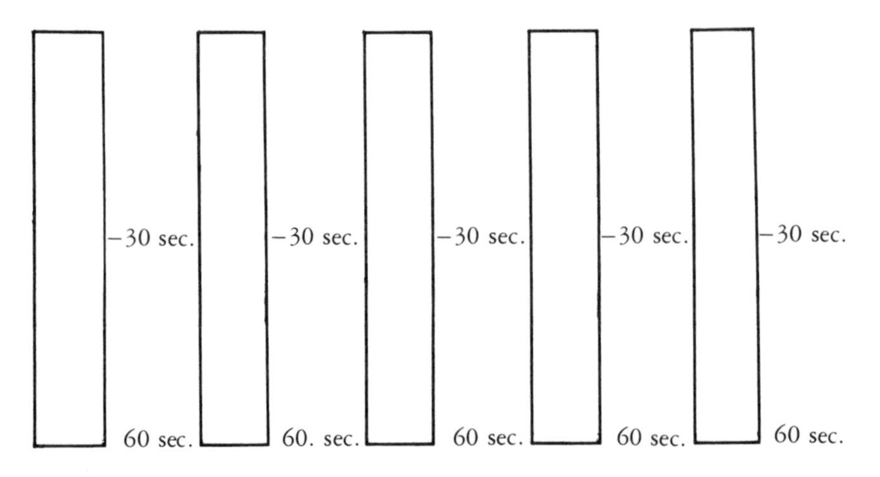

Observation Instrument Format Design

The creation of self-made observation forms requires the teacher to carefully consider how often the observation instrument will be used. The teacher will also need to consider how often the specific behaviors will be recorded (e.g., every time they occur, every 3 seconds, every 30 seconds, at 3-minute intervals).

Once the teacher decides how often the information will be collected, he or she can design the observation form. Checklists, tallies, or various coding systems can be developed. No one format is preferable. Experimentation and actual use of the observation instrument will reveal the kind of format that is most desirable.

The design and use of self-made observation forms is one of the most complex steps in teacher self-assessment. The following is a summary of the activities involved in observation form development:

1. Identify the behaviors that will be observed.
2. Examine a number of expert-prepared instruments to get an idea of the design of observation instruments. The expert-prepared observation forms will assist in determining (1) the type of form to be designed, (2) techniques for identifying behavior, and (3) methods for interpreting and analyzing collected information.
3. Construct the observation form to illustrate one or more of these facets: (1) identification of a specific behavior, (2) the frequency of a behavior, and (3) the sequence of behaviors. Design the directions and format for actual data collection.
4. Audiotape or videotape a classroom session; analyze data in terms of how well the classroom interaction was collected.
5. Revise the observation form on the basis of the findings, record another classroom session, and use this recording to collect data on the revised form.

The creation of observation forms is an important but complex part of self-assessment practices. The development of self-made forms requires more time and patience than all other steps in teacher self-assessment. Some teachers will prefer expert-prepared observation forms; others will find the self-made observation forms more beneficial. It is not uncommon in self-assessment for teachers to use both expert-prepared and self-made observation forms.

PRINCIPLES OF TEACHER SELF-ASSESSMENT

Recognizing and understanding the purposes of teacher self-assessment is a prerequisite to successful self-help practices. Essentially, this process is embodied in the basic Seven Steps of Teacher Self-Assessment. In addition to these steps, there is a set of principles that guide the teacher through each step in self-assessment (see Figure 7). These principles must be understood and practiced by teachers engaged in self-assessment.

Engage in Self-Assessment Slowly

Teacher self-assessment is a practice designed to occur over a long period of time. Self-help should not be viewed as a strategy that is going to revolutionize teacher practices in one or two applications. For many people, self-assessment can be an intimidating process. To approach self-help with a positive attitude requires careful preparation and deliberate forethought. A steady, common-sense approach to the use of any or all self-assessment steps is necessary for productive self-examination.

Strive for Openness in Self-Assessment

Adopting an attitude of wanting to examine teaching behavior for the purpose of self-improvement is paramount in the initial stages of teacher self-assessment. Being open to change is a state of mind that affects the teacher's actual use of the steps or strategies found in teacher self-assessment. Openness requires teachers to be psychologically prepared for self-examination; teachers must be able to look at both their strengths and their weaknesses. Equally important, teachers must guard against using any form of rationalization to explain away characteristics of their teaching that are not favorable or positive.

Focus on a Small Number of Instructional Skills

The study of teaching is extremely complex. As a consequence, a teacher just beginning self-assessment can become overwhelmed by looking at his or her total teaching performance. For this reason, it is logical to proceed by focusing on only one or two teaching skills during a self-assessment period. As a teacher's confidence builds in the process of self-examination, he or she can study additional skills in the total context of classroom instruction.

Figure 7
AN ORGANIZATIONAL APPROACH TO UNDERSTANDING AND USING TEACHER SELF-ASSESSMENT

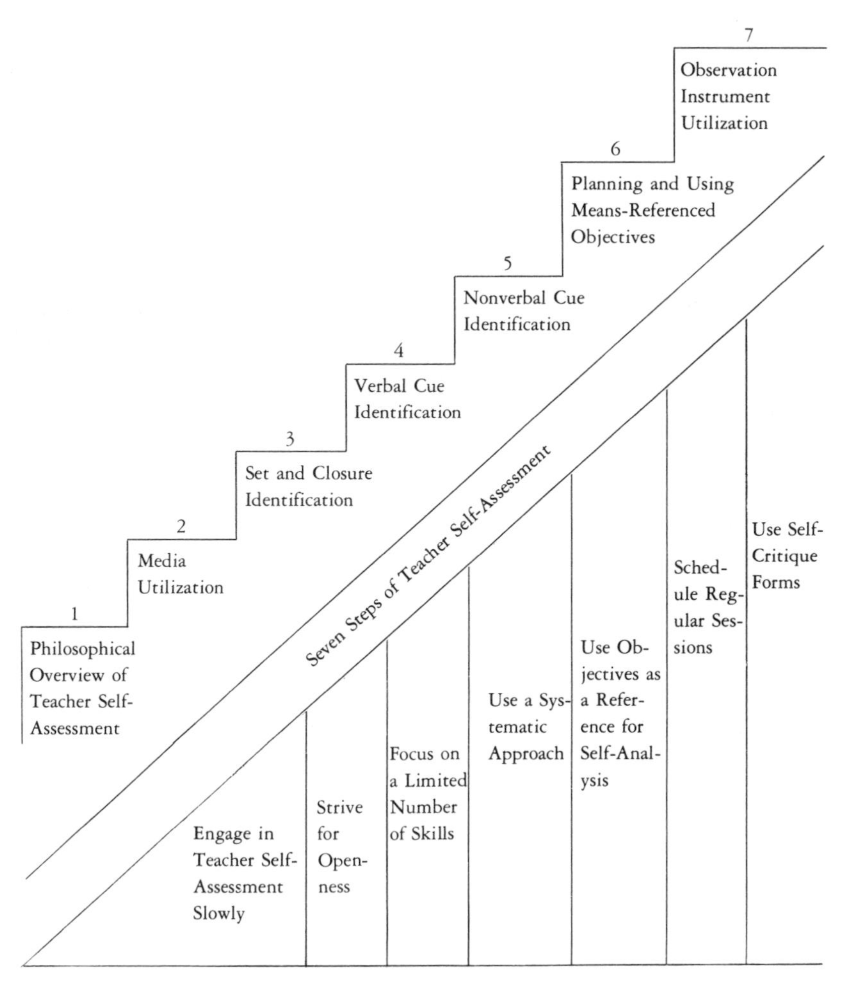

Undergirding Principles of the Seven Steps of Teacher Self-Assessment

Use a Systematic Approach in Self-Help Activities

A simple three stage model can provide direction and focus for the teacher engaging in improvement of instruction. The three basic stages are (1) identify, (2) control, and (3) maintain or modify.

In Stage 1, the teacher engaging in self-assessment begins to examine set, closure, and verbal and nonverbal cues. The purpose is to make the teacher aware of behaviors found in the teaching act. The use of the audiotape and videotape recorder is essential during this stage.

In Stage 2, the teacher begins to concentrate on the relationship between teacher behavior and resultant student behavior. Studying the relationship between teacher behavior and student behavior enables the teacher to arrive at conclusions concerning the "cause and effect" relationship found in classroom interaction. The study of this relationship permits the teacher to learn how to control classroom behaviors. Means-referenced objectives and observation instruments are especially useful during this stage. Learning to control instructional behaviors is inherently more difficult than being aware of what is occurring in the instructional act.

Stage 3 involves decisionmaking on the part of the teacher. This stage is not as time-consuming as the first two stages. During this stage, the teacher arrives at a conclusion concerning those behaviors that are desirable or undesirable in the teaching act. Stage 3 involves maintaining effective teaching behaviors and removing ineffective teaching behaviors.

The teacher just beginning self-assessment must be careful not to confuse the third stage of the model with the first stage. Changing specific teaching behaviors without total knowledge of the instructional self usually leads to frustration and confusion. Systematic use of the three stage model allows the teacher to proceed logically and systematically in finding out how to improve classroom instruction.

Use Objectives as a Reference for Self-Analysis

Any attempt at self-analysis must be made by comparing performance with the established objectives of the instructional lesson—both instructional objectives and means-referenced objectives. A self-critique without reference to objectives usually results in observing extraneous teaching characteristics. Extraneous teaching characteristics often include such variables as weight gain, hair loss, dress, speech patterns, or classroom conditions, which are irrelevant to the teaching or learning outcomes. These variables may be interesting, but they seldom have a major impact on student behaviors and attitudes. Effective self-examination comes about when a teacher uses a plan that includes instructional and means-referenced objectives as major reference points.

Schedule Regular Sessions for Self-Assessment Practices

An overall schedule that identifies time, place, and activities for self-assessment practices can prove to be an important feature in the successful implementation of these practices. Developing the self-discipline needed to schedule self-analysis is often difficult. Self-analysis can be time-consuming and is often perceived by teachers as less urgent than other educational obligations.

Productive, long-term self-assessment practices occur when the teacher learns to chart regular sessions for self-help activities. With regular schedules, comes routine. Routine soon becomes habit, and the more self-assessment practices are employed, the more the classroom teacher realizes their value. Daily, weekly, or monthly schedules created for self-assessment activities are of utmost importance.

Use Self-Critique Forms for Recording Self-Assessment Plans and Findings

Self-critique forms provide a written record of the teacher's self-assessment activities. They are completely different from the observation instruments described earlier. They are a method of documenting the specifics of the entire self-analysis process (e.g., time, date, methods of analysis). Teachers can easily design self-critique forms by establishing a format that suits their individual needs. The format of the self-critique sheet will vary according to the teacher's preferences, the stage of self-examination the teacher is engaged in, and the type of observation instruments the teacher employs to collect classroom information. Effective self-assessment activities begin and end with the use of a self-critique form. A sample self-critique form is depicted in Figure 8. The form illustrates how many of the concepts dealt with in the Seven Steps of Self-Assessment can be incorporated in a self-critique form.

The undergirding principles of teacher self-assessment help give the Seven Steps of Self-Assessment purpose and direction. These principles assist teachers in viewing the seven steps as a series of options that can be selected according to individual needs. No one step is an effective plan of self-help by itself. The selection of a combination of several of the steps coupled with an overall knowledge of how to use them gives structure to the practice of self-assessment.

Figure 8
SELF-CRITIQUE FORM

Name ______________________ Date __________

Class ________________ Topic ________________

Critique Session 1 2 3 4 5 6 7 8 9 10

Strategy of Observation: ______________________

____

Goals or Instructional Objectives (Student Objectives)

1. ____

2. ____

3. ____

4. ____

Means-Referenced Objectives (Teacher Objectives)

1. ____

2. ____

3. ____

4. ____

Observation Tools Employed in Observation: ______________

____

____

Observation Notes: ______________________________

____

____

Major Conclusions: ______________________________

____

Projected Next Area of Study: ____________________

____

Scheduled Date for Next Observation: ______________

References

Amidon, Edmund J., and Flanders, Ned A. *The Role of the Teacher in the Classroom: A Manual for Understanding and Improving Teacher Classroom Behavior.* Minneapolis: Association for Productive Teaching, 1967, p. 72.

Bailey, Gerald D. "The Relationship Between Classroom Interaction Patterns and Teacher Self-Perception." Unpublished manuscript. Manhattan, Kansas: Kansas State University, 1972.

———. "A Study of Classroom Interaction Patterns from Student Teaching to Independent Classroom Practices." Doctoral dissertation. Lincoln, Nebraska: University of Nebraska, 1972.

———. "Improving Classroom Instruction with Student Feedback." *Educational Technology* 17, no. 10 (1978): 39–43.

———. "Teacher Self-Assessment: In Search of a Philosophical Foundation." National Association of Secondary School Principals *Bulletin* 62, no. 422 (1978): 64–70.

———. "A Follow-up Survey of Teachers Trained in Self-Assessment Competencies." Unpublished manuscript. Manhattan, Kansas: Kansas State University, 1980, p. 3.

———. "Set and Closure Revisited." National Association of Secondary School Principals *Bulletin* 64, no. 435 (1980): 103–110.

———, and Lux, John E. "A Programmed Approach to the Teaching of the Instructional Analysis System." Unpublished manuscript. Lincoln, Nebraska: University of Nebraska, 1972.

Brophy, Jere E., and Evertson, Carolyn M. *Learning from Teaching: A Developmental Perspective.* Boston: Allyn and Bacon, 1976.

Centra, John. *Determining Faculty Effectiveness.* San Francisco: Jossey-Bass, 1979.

Flanders, Ned A. *Analyzing Teacher Behavior.* Reading, Mass.: Addison-Wesley, 1970.

Fuller, F.F., and Manning, B.A. "Self-Confrontation Reviewed: A Conceptualization for Video Playback in Teacher Education." *Review of Educational Research* 43, no. 4 (1973): 469–528.

———, Veldman, D.J.; and Richek, H.G. "Tape Recordings, Feedback and Prospective Teachers' Self Evaluation." *Alberta Journal of Educational Research* 12 (1966): 301–7.

Goodlad, J.I., et al. *Behind the Classroom Door.* Worthington, Ohio: C.A. Jones, 1970.

Hook, Colin M., and Rosenshine, Barak. "Accuracy of Teacher Reports of Their Classroom Behaviors." *Review of Educational Research* 49, no. 1 (1979): 1–12.

Kaplan, Robert M., and Pascoe, Gregory C. "Humorous Lectures and Humorous Examples: Some Effects upon Comprehension and Retention." *Journal of Educational Psychology* 69, no. 1 (1977): 61–65.

Levin, Benjy. "Teacher Evaluation—A Review of Research." *Educational Leadership* 37, no. 3 (1979): 240–45.

Lux, John E., and Bailey, Gerald D. "Instructional Analysis System." Unpublished manuscript, University of Nebraska, 1972.

MacGraw, F.M., Jr. "The Use of the 35mm Time Lapse Photography as a Feedback and Observation Instrument in Teacher Education." Doctoral dissertation, Stanford University, 1966. Ann Arbor, Mich.: University Microfilms.

McNeil, John, and Popham, James. "The Assessment of Teacher Competence." In *Second Handbook of Research on Teaching,* edited by Robert M.W. Travers. Chicago: Rand McNally, 1973, pp. 218–44.

Marks, James R.; Stoops, Emery; and King-Stoops, Joyce. *Handbook of Educational Supervision: A Guide for the Practitioner.* Boston: Allyn and Bacon, 1971.

Medley, Don M. "The Effectiveness of Teachers." In *Research on Teaching: Concepts, Findings, and Implications,* edited by Penelope L. Peterson and Herbert J. Walberg. Berkeley, Calif.: McCutchan, 1979.

Miller, Patrick W. *Nonverbal Communication.* Washington, D.C.: National Education Association, 1981.

Morse, K.R.; Kysilka, M.L.; and Davis, M.L., Jr. *Effects of Different Types of Supervisory Feedback on Teacher Candidates' Development of Refocusing Behaviors.* R and D Report Series no. 48. Austin: University of Texas, Research and Development Center for Teacher Education, 1970.

Neely, John. In *A Review of Research on Teacher Education,* edited by Levon Balzer. Columbus: ERIC/SMEAC, 1973.

Peck, Robert F., and Tucker, James A. "Research on Teacher Education. In *Second Handbook of Research on Teaching,* edited by Robert M.W. Travers. Chicago: Rand McNally, 1973.

Peterson, Penelope L., and Walberg, Herbert J., eds. *Research on Teaching: Concepts, Findings and Implications.* Berkeley, Calif.: McCutchan, 1979.

Rosenshine, Barak, and Furst, Norma. "The Use of Direct Observation to Study Teaching." In *Second Handbook of Research on Teaching,* edited by Robert M.W. Travers. Chicago: Rand McNally, 1973, pp. 122–83.

Rowe, Mary Budd. "Wait-Time and Rewards as Instructional Variables, Their Influence on Language, Logic, and Fate Control. Part I. Wait-Time." *Journal of Research in Science Teaching* 11 (1974): 81–94.

Soar, Robert. "Teaching Behavior Related to Pupil Growth." *International Review of Education* 18 (1972): 508–26.

Solomon, D., and Kendall, A.J. *Final Report: Individual Characteristics and Children's Performance in Varied Educational Settings.* Rockville, Md.: Montgomery County Public Schools, 1976.

Steele, J.M.; House, F.R.; and Kerins, T. "An Instrument for Assessing Instructional Climate Through Low-Influence Student Judgments." *American Educational Research Journal* 8 (1971): 447–66.

Sullivan, Cheryl Granade. *Clinical Supervision: A State of the Art Review.* Washington, D.C.: Association for Supervision and Curriculum Development, 1980, pp. 1–47.

Tuckman, B.W.; McCall, K.M.; and Hyman, R.T. "The Modification of Teacher Behavior: Effects of Dissonance and Coded Feedback." *American Educational Research Journal* 6 (1969): 607–19.

Urback, Floyd D. "A Study of Recurring Patterns of Teaching." Doctoral dissertation, University of Nebraska, 1966.

Valentine, Jerry. "The Supervisory Process—A Practical Look." National Association of Secondary School Principals *Bulletin* 62, no. 422 (December 1978): 55–59.

Walberg, H.J., and Thomas, S.C. "Open Education: An Operational Definition and Validation in Great Britain and the United States." *American Educational Research Journal* 9 (1972): 197–207.

Weiss, J. *Validating and Improving Instruments for Describing Openness of School Programs.* Toronto: Ontario Institute for Studies in Education, 1973.

Wiles, Jon, and Bondi, Joseph. *Supervision, A Guide to Practice.* Columbus, Ohio: Charles E. Merrill, 1980.

Wood, Peter. *Teacher Evaluation: Feedback to Improve Teaching.* ERIC ED 139 733, 1976.

BIBLIOGRAPHY

Teacher Self-Assessment

Bailey, Gerald D. "A Follow-up Survey of Teachers Trained in Self-Assessment Competencies." Unpublished paper, Kansas State University, 1980.

______. "Improving Classroom Instruction: Is There a Better Model?" National Association of Secondary School Principals *Bulletin* 62, no. 414 (January 1978): 50–59.

______. "Improving Classroom Instruction with Means-Referenced Objectives." *Educational Technology* 17, no. 7 (July 1977): 13–15.

______. "Improving Classroom Instruction with Student Feedback." *Educational Technology* 17, no. 10 (October 1978): 39–43.

______. "Maximizing the Potential of the Videotape Recorder in Teacher Self-Assessment." *Instructional Technology* 19, no. 9 (September 1979): 39–44.

______. "Self-Made Observation Instruments: An Aid to Self-Assessment." *Educational Technology* 17, no. 3 (March 1977): 49–51.

______. "Set and Closure Revisited." National Association of Secondary School Principals *Bulletin* 64, no. 435 (April 1980): 103–10.

______. "Student Self-Assessment: Helping Students Help Themselves." Kappa Delta Pi *Record* 15, no. 3 (February 1979): 86–88, 96.

______. "Teacher Self-Assessment: In Search of a Philosophical Foundation." National Association of Secondary School Principals *Bulletin* 62, no. 422 (December 1978): 64–70.

______. "Teacher Self-Assessment: A Teacher-Student Chain." Kappa Delta Pi *Record* 15, no. 2 (December 1977): 48–50.

______, and Scott, Robert E. "How to Use Trainee Feedback to Improve Trainer Behavior." *Training Magazine* 16, no. 4 (April 1979): 28–29.

Media

Ellett, Lowell E., and Smith, Earl P. "Improving Performance of Classroom Teachers Through Videotaping and Self-Evaluation." *Audiovisual Communication Review* 23, no. 3 (Fall 1975): 277–88.

Fuller, F. F., and Manning, B.A. "Self-Confrontation Reviewed: A Conceptualization for Video Playback in Teacher Education." *Review of Educational Research* 43, no. 4 (1973): 469–528.

______; Veldman, D.J.; and Richek, H.G. "Tape Recordings, Feedback and Prospective Teachers' Self Evaluation." *Alberta Journal of Educational Research* 12 (1966); 301–7.

McGrady, Seamus. "Smile, You're on Classroom Camera." *Nation's Schools* 92, no. 4 (October 1973): 44–46.

MacGraw, F. M., Jr. "The Use of the 35mm Time Lapse Photography as a Feedback and Observation Instrument in Teacher Education." Doctoral dissertation, Stanford University 1966. Ann Arbor, Mich: University Microfilms, 1966.

Peck, Robert F., and Tucker, James A. "Research on Teacher Education." In *Second Handbook of Research on Teaching,* edited by Robert M. W. Travers. Chicago: Rand McNally, 1973, pp. 940–78.

Salomon, G., and McDonald F. J. "Pre-Test and Post-Test Reactions to Self-Viewing One's Teaching Performance on Videotape." *Journal of Educational Psychology* 61 (1970): 280–86.

Verbal Communication

Bailey, Gerald D. "The Relationship Between Classroom Interaction Patterns and Teacher Self-Perception." Unpublished paper, Kansas State University, 1972.

———. "A Study of Classroom Interaction Patterns from Student Teaching to Independent Classroom Practices." Doctoral dissertation, University of Nebraska, 1972. (Ann Arbor, Michigan: University Microfilms, 1972)

——— and Lux, John E. "A Programmed Approach to the Teaching of the Instructional Analysis System." Unpublished paper, University of Nebraska, 1972.

Kaplan, Robert M., and Pascoe, Gregory C. "Humorous Lectures and Humorous Examples: Some Effects upon Comprehension and Retention." *Journal of Educational Psychology* 69, no. 1 (1977): 61–65.

Lux, John E., and Bailey, Gerald D. "Instructional Analysis System." Unpublished paper, University of Nebraska, 1972.

Medley, Don M. "The Effectiveness of Teachers." In *Research on Teaching: Concepts, Findings, and Implications,* edited by Penelope L. Peterson and Herbert J. Walberg. Berkeley, Calif.: McCutchan, 1979; pp. 11–27.

Peterson, Penelope L., and Walberg, Herbert J. eds. *Research on Teaching: Concepts, Findings, and Implications.* Berkeley, Calif: McCutchan, 1979.

Soar, Robert. "Teaching Behavior Related to Pupil Growth." *International Review of Education* 18 (1972): 508–26.

Urback, Floyd D. "A Study of Recurring Patterns of Teaching." Doctoral dissertation, University of Nebraska, 1966.

Nonverbal Communication

Amidon, Peggy. *Nonverbal Interaction Analysis: A Method of Systematically Observing and Recording Nonverbal Behavior.* Minneapolis: Association for Productive Teaching, 1971.

Galloway, Charles. *Teaching Is Communicating: Nonverbal Language in the Classroom.* Bulletin no. 29. Washington, D. C.: Association for Student Teaching, 1970.

______. "Nonverbal Communication in Teaching." In *Teaching: Vantage Points for Study,* edited by R. T. Hyman. 2d ed. Philadelphia: Lippincott, 1974.

Knapp, Mark L. *Nonverbal Communication in Human Interaction.* New York: Holt, Rinehart and Winston, 1978.

Miller, Patrick W. *Nonverbal Communication.* Washington, D.C. National Education Association, 1981.

Morris, Desmond. *Manwatching: A Field Guide to Human Behavior.* New York: Harry N. Abrams, 1977.

Rowe, Mary Budd. "Wait-Time and Rewards as Instructional Variables, Their Influence on Language, Logic, and Fate Control. Part I. Wait-Time." *Journal of Research in Science Teaching* 11 (1974): 81–94.

Smith, Howard A. "Nonverbal Communication in Teaching." *Review of Educational Research* 49, no. 4 (Fall 1979): 631–72.

Goals and Objectives

Bloom, Benjamin S. et al., eds. *Taxonomy of Educational Objectives: The Classification of Educational Goals,* Handbook I. New York: Longman, 1956.

Harrow, Anita J. *A Taxonomy of the Psychomotor Domain.* New York: McKay, 1964.

Krathwohl, D. R.; Bloom, Benjamin; and Masia, Bertram. *Taxonomy of Educational Objectives, Handbook II: Affective Domain.* New York: McKay, 1964.

Mager, Robert F. *Preparing Instructional Objectives.* Belmont, Calif.: Fearon, 1962.

Tyler, Ralph. *Basic Principles of Curriculum and Instruction.* Chicago: University of Chicago Press, 1949.

Observation Instruments

Amidon, Edmund J., and Hough, John B., eds. *Interaction Analysis: Theory, Research, and Application.* Reading, Mass.: Addison-Wesley Publishing Co., 1967.

Brophy, Jere E., and Evertson, Carolyn M. *Learning from Teaching: A Developmental Perspective.* Boston: Allyn and Bacon, 1976.

Flanders, Ned A. *Analyzing Teacher Behavior.* Reading Mass.: Addison-Wesley, 1970.

Rosenshine, Barak, and Furst, Norma. "The Use of Direct Observation to Study Teaching." In *Second Handbook of Research on Teaching,* edited by Robert M. W. Travers. Chicago: Rand McNally, 1973; pp. 122–83.

Soar, Robert S. "Teacher-Pupil Interaction." In *A New Look at Progressive Education* edited by James R. Squire. Washington, D. C.: Association for Supervision and Curriculum Development Yearbook, 1972; pp. 166–204.

General Interest

Balzer, Levon, ed. *A Review of Research on Teacher Behavior.* Columbus, Ohio: ERIC/SMEAC, 1973.

Becker, Wesley C.; Engelmann, Siegfried; and Thomas, Don R. *Instructor's Manual for Teaching: A Course in Applied Psychology.* Chicago: Science Research Associates, 1971.

Centra, John. *Determining Faculty Effectiveness.* San Francisco: Jossey-Bass, 1979.

Curwin, Richard L., and Fuhrmann, Barbara Schneider. *Discovering Your Teaching Self.* Englewood Cliffs, N.J.: Prentice-Hall, 1975.

Ellett, L. E. "Self-Analysis: Technique for Modifying Teacher Performance in the Teaching/Learning Process." Doctoral dissertation, University of Virginia, 1974.

Flatter, Charles, H., and Koopman, Elizabeth J. "An Inservice Self-Study Program: The Forgotten Key to Educational Success." *Journal of Teacher Education* 27, no. 2 (Summer 1976): 116–18.

Goldhammer, Robert. *Clinical Supervision: Special Methods for the Supervision of Teachers.* New York: Holt, Rinehart and Winston, 1969.

Goodlad, J. I., et al. *Behind the Classroom Door.* Worthington, Ohio: C. A. Jones, 1970.

Hilgard, Ernest R., and Bower, Gordon H. *Theories of Learning.* 4th ed. Englewood Cliffs, N.J.: Prentice-Hall, 1975.

Hook, Colin M., and Rosenshine, Barak. "Accuracy of Teacher Reports of Their Classroom Behaviors." *Review of Educational Research* 49, no. 1 (Winter 1979): 1–12.

Levin, Benjy. "Teacher Evaluation—A Review of Research." *Educational Leadership* 37, no. 3 (December 1979): 240–45.

McNeil, John, and Popham, James. "The Assessment of Teacher Competence." In *Second Handbook of Research on Teaching,* edited by Robert M. W. Travers. Chicago: Rand McNally, 1973; pp. 218–44.

Marks, James R., Stoops, Emery; and King-Stoops, Joyce. *Handbook of Educational Supervision: A Guide for the Practitioner.* Boston: Allyn and Bacon, 1971.

Morse, K. R.; Kysilka, M.L.; and Davis, M.L., Jr. *Effects of Different Types of Supervisory Feedback on Teacher Candidates' Development of Refocusing Behaviors.* R and D Report Series no. 48, Austin: University of Texas, Research and Development Center for Teacher Education, 1970.

Natriello, Gary. *A Summary of Recent Literature on the Evaluation of Principals, Teachers, and Students.* ERIC ED 141 407, 1977.

Neely, John. In *A Review of Research on Teacher Education,* edited by Levon Balzer. Columbus, Ohio: ERIC/SMEAC, 1973.

Riley, Roberta D., and Schaffer, Eugene C. "Self-Certification: Accounting to Oneself." *Journal of Teacher Education* 30, no. 2 (March-April 1979): 23–26.

Solomon, D., and Kendall, A.J. *Final Report: Individual Characteristics and Children's Performance in Varied Educational Settings.* Rockville, Md.: Montgomery County Public Schools, 1976.

Steele, J. M.; House, F. R.; and Kerins, T. "An Instrument for Assessing Instructional Climate Through Low-Influence Student Judgments." *American Educational Research Journal* 8 (1971): 447–66.

Sullivan, Cheryl Granade. *Clinical Supervision: A State of the Art Review.* Washington, D.C.: Association for Supervision and Curriculum Development, 1980.

Tuckman, B. W.; McCall, K.M.; and Hyman, R.T. "The Modification of Teacher Behavior: Effects of Dissonance and Coded Feedback." *American Educational Research Journal* 6 (1969): 607–19.

Valentine, Jerry. "The Supervisory Process—A Practical Look." National Association of Secondary School Principals *Bulletin* 62, no. 422 (December 1978): 55–59.

Walberg, H. J., and Thomas, S. C. "Open Education: An Operational Definition and Validation in Great Britain and the United States." *American Ecucational Research Journal* 9 (1972): 197–207.

Weiss, J. *Validating and Improving Instruments for Describing Openness of School Programs.* Toronto: Ontario Institute for Studies in Education. 1973.

Wiles, Jon, and Bondi, Joseph. *Supervision, A Guide to Practice.* Columbus, Ohio: Charles E. Merrill, 1980.

Wolf, Robert. "How Teachers Feel Toward Evaluation." In *School Evaluation,* edited by Ernest Haus. Berkeley, Calif.: McCutchan, 1973.

Wood, Peter. *Teacher Evaluation: Feedback to Improve Teaching.* ERIC ED 139 733, 1976.